ON REFLECTION

Also by Richard Holloway

Let God Arise (1972)
New Vision of Glory (1974)
A New Heaven (1979)
Beyond Belief (1981)
Signs of Glory (1982)
The Killing (1984)
The Anglican Tradition (ed.) (1984)
Paradoxes of Christian Faith and Life (1984)
The Sidelong Glance (1985)
The Way of the Cross (1986)
Seven to Flee, Seven to Follow (1986)
Crossfire: Faith and Doubt in an Age of Certainty (1988)
The Divine Risk (ed.) (1990)
Another Country, Another King (1991)
Who Needs Feminism? (ed.) (1991)
Anger, Sex, Doubt and Death (1992)
The Stranger in the Wings (1994)
Churches and How to Survive Them (1994)
Behold Your King (1995)
Limping Towards the Sunrise (1996)
Dancing on the Edge (1997)
Godless Morality: Keeping Religion Out of Ethics (1999)
Doubts and Loves: What Is Left of Christianity (2001)
On Forgiveness: How Can We Forgive the Unforgiveable? (2002)
Looking in the Distance: The Human Search for Meaning (2004)
How to Read the Bible (2006)
Between the Monster and the Saint:
Reflections on the Human Condition (2008)
Leaving Alexandria: A Memoir of Faith and Doubt (2012)
A Little History of Religion (2016)
Waiting for the Last Bus (2018)
Stories We Tell Ourselves (2020)
The Heart of Things (2021)

ON REFLECTION

LOOKING FOR LIFE'S MEANING

RICHARD HOLLOWAY

CANONGATE

First published in Great Britain in 2021
by Canongate Books Ltd, 14 High Street, Edinburgh EH1 1TE

canongate.co.uk

1

Copyright © Richard Holloway, 2024

The right of Richard Holloway to be identified as the
author of this work has been asserted by him in accordance
with the Copyright, Designs and Patents Act 1988

Every effort has been made to trace copyright holders and obtain
their permission for the use of copyright material. The publisher
apologises for any errors or omissions and would be grateful if
notified of any corrections that should be incorporated in future
reprints or editions of this book.

British Library Cataloguing-in-Publication Data
A catalogue record for this book is available on
request from the British Library

ISBN 978 1 80530 291 9

Typeset in Garamond MT Std by Palimpsest Book Production Ltd,
Falkirk, Stirlingshire

Printed and bound by CPI Group (UK) Ltd,
Croydon CR0 4YY

For Ian Paton

CONTENTS

Preface ix

1. THE ABSENCE OF GOD — 1
2. THE POLITICS OF FORGIVENESS — 10
3. WHERE ALL THE LADDERS START — 16
4. AUDEN: THE POET PREACHER — 32
5. THE CALEDONIAN ANTISYZYGY — 38
6. AT REQUIEM MASS IN THE USHER HALL — 55
7. THOSE FALLEN LADDERS AGAIN — 61
8. WALKING AWAY FROM CHURCH — 72
9. EXILE — 80
10. SECULAR FAITH — 95
11. GRIEF — 109
12. CREATING HELL — 123
13. IN MEMORIAM — 131
14. MESSIAEN: QUATTUOR POUR LA FIN DU TEMPS — 139
15. THE MUTILATED WORLD — 144
16. A SECULAR SOCIETY — 154
17. DARWIN AND THE BIBLE — 167

ON REFLECTION

18	IMPROVISING ETHICS	174
19	HAS FAITH A FUTURE?	188
20	ARE CHRISTIANS ALLOWED TO BE GAY?	192
21	THIS IS IT	205
22	LISTENING	213
23	KEEPING ON KEEPING CHRISTMAS	217
24	THANKING	225
	Notes	229
	Permission Credits	237

PREFACE

'*On reflection*' is a modest phrase that's had a revolutionary impact on both individuals and societies. It is because we are reflective creatures that we have been able to banish some of the worst evils in our history.

On reflection, we decided in Britain in the early part of the twentieth century that it was both absurd and immoral to deny women the right to vote in parliamentary elections, so they got the vote in 1918.

On reflection, the Church of England decided that it was both absurd and immoral to deny women entry into its priesthood, so it started ordaining them in 1994.

And there are grimmer examples to think about. For most of history, we thought it was moral to enslave other humans, which is why ten million Africans were put on ships and sent to work on plantations in the southern states of the USA, till the slave trade was finally abolished in 1865. This is why former US president Barack Obama described slavery as America's original sin.

And what is true of societies is also true of individuals: they change their minds as well. In a long life, on reflection, I have changed my mind about many things: here are some examples.

I

THE ABSENCE OF GOD

I love the story about the composer who played his latest composition for a friend. When he finished there was a brief silence; then, uneasily, his friend asked: 'What does it mean?' The composer looked at him, said nothing, turned back to the piano – and played it again.

The story points up two important matters. The first is the way we tend to privilege words in the sphere of meaning, something the composer challenged by refusing to translate one form of expression – music – into another, language. I have to confess that I suffer from this kind of prejudice for words myself. I find it hard to grasp the meaning of things unless they are worded for me, put into language. I take this prejudice into art galleries when I go to look at pictures. Not content with *looking* and letting the art disclose its own meaning to me in its own way, I dive immediately for the label beside the painting to find out what I'm looking at. Until I get something in writing I am uneasy: picture has to become word before I know how to interact with it. This is a weakness I am trying to correct, but it is not easy after a lifetime addicted to words. I am learning to look, so that pictures can disclose their meaning to me unmediated by language. I find it hard, yet I know that some of the keenest human experiences are beyond any words to describe. That's why the American painter Edward Hopper said if he could say it he wouldn't have to paint it. Take the feeling of loneliness as an example. It's not easy to communicate it in words, but artists like Hopper have painted it with heart-breaking clarity. You look at a Hopper painting and feel the loneliness penetrate you like a sliver of ice.

Music can do this as well. Take the experience of loss and sadness, and think of music you know that has swept over you like a wave of sorrow. The unsayable, wordlessly expressed with almost unbearable intensity. So, even if we love language, as I do, and wonder at its ability to touch our souls to the quick – and even if we think it is still the best means through which to express our most precious emotions and recognitions – we have to admit there is a problem with some of the claims that have been made for it, which brings me to the second matter.

When thinking about the limitations of language, philosophers talk about the problem of *equivalence*, which goes something like this: because of the special position language holds in our culture, we think we ought to be able to put everything into words, make words equivalent to other realities. We think that if we can say it, we can understand it. But there is no exact verbal equivalence to even the most prosaic item. Words are the names we give things, the signs we create to point to them, but the things themselves are not what we say they are: the word water is not drinkable, nor is the word bread edible. Writers who work with language as their chosen medium know these limitations better than anyone. All the time they are trying to get beyond the words to communicate the experience that lies behind them. That's why the guiding mantra for writers is, 'Show, don't tell.' Show me your hero is charming, don't *tell* me he is; demonstrate the courage of your heroine, don't *tell* me she's brave. Get as close as you can to giving the reader the experience you are trying to describe. Go beyond the words, get through them to the reality, to the experience you are trying to communicate.

Now if this is difficult at the innate level, the level that is available to our senses, then it is infinitely more difficult at the level beyond the physical, where we locate the possibility of the mystery we call God. We experience a double difficulty here. Even if we accept the limitations of language for everyday things; even when we accept that the word 'water' is not itself water; we also know that, even if words failed us and we lost the power of thought, we could at least go on drinking the reality we call water. The *substance* is available to our senses, even if we accept that no word can capture its essence and importance to us. Well, God is not like any other reality. Even for believers, God is not available to their senses the way water is. Of course, you may be going through the desert without water, but even then, you know that water exists somewhere; that you have drunk it, bathed in it, and now remember it with desperate longing.

It is not like that with God and never has been. As far as our senses go, God has always been absent, never been there in the way we know there is water somewhere. That's why we invented a word to express the possibility of an ultimate reality beyond anything we could touch or experience: the word is *transcendent*, which suggests the possibility of that which lies beyond any human understanding or experience.

The puzzle that gnaws at our minds is how to explain the fact that there are facts, that there is something rather than nothing. We can experience the physical universe, touch it, drink it, name it; but we cannot actually find words to account for where or how it came to pass, because there is no *there* there to point at and name. Since we are not very good at living with uncertainties and mysteries, two attempts have been made to resolve the situation, neither very satisfactory. Since we cannot get outside the universe to account for it, we postulate possible solutions to the mystery of its existence. One answer, prominent at the moment, says it is self-created and popped out of nothing. Since it is hard to get your head around that idea, scientists offer a term to fill the gap, borrowed from mathematics, called a 'singularity'. Singularities are unknowns that defy the current understanding of physics; infinitely small, infinitely dense *somethings*, from which everything has emerged. Being the indefatigable explorers they are, it is not hard to imagine that one day scientists will find out more about this vanishingly complex hypothesis; but even if they manage to nail it down and tell us more about it, they'll still have to account for *it*, say something about where it came from. We'll inevitably have to ask them this question: if the universe came out of *this*, where did *this* come out of?

It was to avoid that infinite regression that we came up with another possible explanation, the one we coined the word transcendent to point to. Beyond the material realm, it is suggested, there must be a non-material, self-conscious intelligence that caused the physical universe to be. And 'God' is the name we have given to that hypothesis. But even this apparently powerful causal option offers no escape from dizzying regression, because even God is open to the naive challenge: 'Mummy, who made God?' This is actually a good question, and one to which no really satisfactory answer has been given. The classical answer is what philosophers would call meaning by definition: God, the reply goes, is self-caused and self-existent – that's what God means. God is the uncaused cause, the unmade maker, the uncreated creator. But by offering those modifiers you have not actually added any new information; you've just built the answer to the question into the definition of the term God. This is like the doctor in Molière who, when asked how opium induced sleep, replied that it contained a sleepy faculty whose nature is to put people to sleep. Nevertheless, since most people don't like sliding down the slippery slope of endless regression, they build ledges on which to stand with some confidence: either by opting for the possibility that the universe can account for its existence within its own natural integrity; or by opting for the supra-natural or transcendent agency of an intelligence that is outside nature but gives rise to it. In our time the arguments between these two possible explanations are being debated with increased ferocity, probably because neither side is able to deliver the knock-out blow to the other.

My difficulty with this debate is this: if it's tough enough talking about what we have seen, how on earth are we to talk about what we cannot see? This difficulty applies to both ends of the debate about what caused the universe, but recently I have had more trouble at the God end of the debate. I have felt glutted with the verbal promiscuity of religion, and the absolute confidence with which it talks about that which is beyond our knowing. One of the biggest ironies here is that in one of the great Christian poems we are told that God, aware of the inadequacy of words, empties himself of language and becomes flesh, becomes that which is available to our senses: a life. Yet along comes what E.M. Forster described as poor little talkative Christianity and turns flesh back into words again, trillions of them, poured out incessantly from pulpits, books and on the airwaves, reducing the mystery of that which is beyond all utterance into chatter. I mind religious verbal over-confidence more than I mind its atheistic opposite, because atheists are not claiming to put ultimate reality into words. Speaking entirely personally, and without wanting to generalise or universalise my own struggles, I have to admit that religious language has ceased to be able to convey the mystery of the possibility of God for me. This is precisely *because* it confidently claims to be able to make present that which I only experience as absence, though it is an absence that sometimes feels like a presence, the way the dead – great writers, for instance – sometimes leave an unfading impression on the rooms they spent their lives in.

I don't want to go back to the days when I had to name that absence. Even back then I felt insecure whenever I was called on to offer a description of that great absence. The best I was able to do was to persuade myself and others to choose to live as if the absence contained a

THE ABSENCE OF GOD

presence that was unconditionally loving. That possible identification, I thought, was surely worth betting my shirt on. But it came as a relief when I was able to name my belief as an emptiness that I was no longer prepared to fill with words.

But though I lost the explanatory words for it, probably forever, sometimes that absence came without word to me in a showing that did not tell. So it is now the absence of God I want to wait with and be faithful to. In this determination I have been helped by the words of a thinker and mystic who herself mistrusted words about God, Simone Weil. A few years ago, an Australian poet called James Charlton sent me a poem he had written about a time in Weil's life when she worked in a vineyard; the poem contains quotations from her notebooks and journals. Poets, paradoxically, use words to take us beyond words into a silence that can itself be the experience of absence. I want to end with his poem, because it took me beyond words into that absence that may even be a kind of presence . . .

> She bends in opaque light, in heat-blaze;
> picks grapes, prunes thoughts and words.
> A hare crouches near the vines:
> fully attentive, no muscular effort,
> no brow-wrinkling concentration.
>
> The vines' silent liturgy: stem, branch,
> stalk, leaf. Attend the planet's rhythm, repeat
> the Rhône Valley's quiet recitation of pure grape,
> nine hours each day.

ON REFLECTION

In borrowed cape and boots, Simone
pursues her life's anomaly: to crave for less,
achieve peace with loss of all sense
of presence. *Truth is conveyed by what is withheld.*

Attend, recite, repeat: stem, stalk, sap.
She picks her way into autumn,
the body's rhythm. Snip this tangle,
snap tendril; shift away from words.
A brace of ravens waddles down a furrow,
lunges at each songbird. Nature's daily work;
truth of world as is.

*I'd rather be an atheist with passion
for Earth than a consoled Christian.*
Give up self-questioning, abandon
the search. Relinquish the mind's
mythographic cast. Accept the void
of letting-be.

*It is not for me to seek, or even to believe
in God. I have only to refuse belief
in gods that are not God.*

Each pilgrim vine is circumscribed yet wayward;
each cluster blazing purple in light,
cold black in shade.
*A matter of seeing deeper, penetrating truth.
Only the lived reality has point.*

THE ABSENCE OF GOD

Can trellises entwine the vine?
Then excise all belief: face emptiness.
Expose the mesh of long-held shibboleths;
defy the grid imposed upon
the world's real labour.[1]

2

THE POLITICS OF FORGIVENESS

In an unpublished novel, my late friend John Whale describes one of the most difficult of human predicaments. Philip, the main character in the story, has gone into the country near Oxford to prepare for the death that cancer will soon bring to him. His predicament is that he has a sin on his conscience, for which he believes there is no obvious forgiveness. His mother had been a monster of tyranny and intolerance all his life, but towards her end he had taken her into his home to care for till her death. Confused, doubly incontinent and enduringly spiteful, she maintained an iron grip on him and would permit no one else to assist in her care. So he stopped feeding her, giving her, instead, occasional cups of hot water. She hardly noticed, and in a few days she was dead. Now Philip, contemplating his own impending death, is unable to find forgiveness. Who can forgive him? He cannot forgive himself. Though he is a priest, he is not quite sure if there is a God to forgive him; and, anyway, can God forgive on his mother's behalf? This is where the predicament really bites: she who was sinned against is no longer available to offer the forgiveness that might heal his tortured heart.

THE POLITICS OF FORGIVENESS

This is a dramatic example of a not uncommon experience. Many innocent people feel guilt at the death of a loved one: did they do enough, or did their neglect somehow contribute to the tragedy? And the comfort of friends does not really help, because the one person who might make a difference is no longer there to make it. The pain is crueller if something wrong *was* done, if there *was* some kind of culpable neglect. That is when guilt burns and gnaws at the gut and changes the beauty of the day into bleakness and sorrow.

Bad as all this is on the personal level, it is a thousand times worse at the political or collective level where whole communities stare in unforgiving hatred at one another. Who is to do the forgiving there? All the sides have inflicted terrible wounds on one another, so where can the forgiving start? Who is to bring back the dead to speak the words of release and reconciliation? And anyway, wouldn't forgiveness cheapen the lives that have been lost, and diminish the responsibility of those who took them? 'Cheap grace', it has been called, this forgiving of others, this letting them off, this turning the other cheek. They should be brought to account, should pay for it, should burn in hell, should stay in jail till they rot, the voices cry, because they have taken joy away forever from our lives.

Yes, the not-forgiving is understandable, but it is a terrible mirror image of the punishment we mete out to the offenders. It keeps us in prison as well, locked up in our own hatred, endlessly working the treadmill of our own bitter memories. So what can we do about the confusion that surrounds forgiveness? How can we pick our way through it? We would probably all agree that at some stage in the process the offence has to be admitted if the forgiving is to do its work on the one who needs it; surely we can't receive forgiveness till we acknowledge that we need it? Related to that is the ancient human conviction that we are responsible for our own actions, have freedom, could have chosen otherwise. That's what gnaws at us in those times of guilt and remorse when we look back at our lives: a little more self-control here, a slight change of direction there, and things could have been so different – and we would not now be eaten up with regret.

All of that is true, and there could be no moral life if it wasn't true, but it is not the whole truth. The men who hammered the nails into the hands and feet of Jesus must have known what they were doing, must have had some responsibility, yet he prayed, 'Father forgive them, for they know not what they do.' Maybe he just meant the executioners, the ones who did the dirty work, not the real agents of the crime, Pilate and Caiaphas, but I doubt it. I think they were also included in the forgiveness he prayed for on the Friday that Christians call 'Good'. Because, and I think this is what he was getting at, none of us is completely in charge of our lives. To a very great extent we are made what we are by factors that were not in our control. The crushing weight of the past is there behind us, forming and moulding us, so that it is sometimes tempting to believe that our choices are hardly ours at all. Much of what we are comes straight from our animal past. It is true, of course, that consciousness gives us some control over our instincts, but it is far from complete. We all know the experience of moral powerlessness: 'I couldn't help it,' we say, 'something got into me.' If this is true of many of our private choices, think how much truer it is when people get caught up in historical tragedies over which they have no control. If you had a bitter childhood in a Palestinian refugee camp, it might make you what the world calls a terrorist. If you spent your boyhood in the divided streets of Belfast, it might make you into the kind of man who could be persuaded to pick up the gun. We know how formative early childhood experience is in making us into what we later become, for better or for worse. When we think about it, therefore, the human situation is actually quite complicated. Yes, we know we are responsible for our own actions, have free will; but we also know that other people's choices have influenced and helped to form us, so our freedom is a qualified thing at best, and some people have been dealt a hand that hardly offers them any choices.

This is why we have to think again about forgiveness and see how it operates, see just how subtle and profound it is. To begin with, let us leave the offender on one side and notice how important forgiveness is for the healing and growth of the forgiver. If there is no forgiving the original offence just keeps growing and can take over a whole life. This is what happened to a woman in the United States. Her daughter had been murdered, the killer was convicted and waiting execution on death row. The mother hated him with a consuming hatred and planned to be present at his execution, but she also wanted to confront him before his death with what he had done, so she arranged to visit him in prison. As she spoke to him she started crying, found herself forgiving him and a great weight fell from her. She was no longer imprisoned in bitterness and hatred, no longer wanted the killer killed. She continued to visit him and one day, in tears, he confessed his guilt and asked for the forgiveness he had already been given. Now she campaigns against capital punishment and her life has been given back to her.

We should notice one or two things about this case. It was because he had already been forgiven that the killer was able to repent. The forgiveness melted his defences and helped him to see and own his crime for the first time. This is how the radical forgiveness that Jesus taught seems to work: the father of the Prodigal forgives his son before he gets a word out, and it is that act of grace that melts his selfish heart into real repentance. Judge and attack me and I'll defend myself with anger and violence; offer me love and understanding and you'll break my heart into sorrow for the way I've hurt you. Forgiveness can release honesty in the offender; more importantly, it liberates the person who has been offended, so that she is no longer trapped, caught up in the continuing horror of the event, and can move away from it into a new future.

The practice of forgiveness is essential to a healthy private life, but it is just as essential in political life, especially in situations of chronic conflict. Just think of the conflicts that have scarred human history, the consequences of which persist to this day – many of them rooted in religion. The ancient conflict between Shia and Sunni Muslims in the Middle East still dictates the opposing policies of Iran and Saudi Arabia, just as religious conflict continues to dictate the politics of Northern Ireland. Who could ever pick their way through the ancient, complicated antagonisms of Northern Ireland

and produce an accurate check sheet of the rights and wrongs of that tragedy?

What the Good Friday Agreement of 1998 did was to admit the sins of the past, on both sides, but to refuse to let them dictate the future. The philosopher Immanuel Kant said that forgiveness interrupts the past and steers it in a different direction, and by so doing it gives us back the future. That is what happened on that day in 1998. It did not heal the past, but – in Kant's phrase – it interrupted the consequences by steering them in a different direction and allowed the possibility of a different kind of future. Forgiveness gives us the courage to leave unfinished business unfinished, so that we can get on with the rest of our lives.

3

WHERE ALL THE LADDERS START

In his old age the poet W.B. Yeats suffered a crisis over the source of his art. It was more than writer's block, the inability to get the juices flowing that has confronted most people who've ever had to get a quota of words down on a blank sheet of paper; this time it seemed to have more to do with the very origin or authority of his inspiration as a poet. In 'The Circus Animals' Desertion' he sets out the problem:

> I sought a theme and sought for it in vain,
> I sought it daily for six weeks or so.
> Maybe at last being but a broken man
> I must be satisfied with my heart, although
> Winter and summer till old age began
> My circus animals were all on show.[1]

In his note on this poem, Daniel Albright, the late, great Yeats scholar and Professor of Literature at Harvard, tells us that Yeats '. . . once thought that his symbols – the matter of his art – were taken from some celestial public domain',[2] and we know quite a lot about the kind of celestial domain Yeats had in mind. He dabbled in a number of esoteric practices, such as occultism, Rosicrucianism, and spirit-writing. Yet in 'The Circus Animals' Desertion' it had already dawned on Yeats that his art did not have its origins in some occult, celestial domain, but in his own messy humanity. He ends the poem like this:

> Those masterful images because complete
> Grew in pure mind but out of what began?
> A mound of refuse or the sweepings of a street,
> Old kettles, old bottles, and a broken can,
> Old iron, old bones, old rags, that raving slut
> Who keeps the till. Now that my ladder's gone
> I must lie down where all the ladders start
> In the foul rag and bone shop of the heart.[3]

Albright tells us that W.H. Auden used these lines to illustrate the lack of relation 'between the moral quality of a maker's life and the aesthetic value of the works he makes . . . every artist knows that the sources of his art are what Yeats called "the foul rag and bone shop of the heart", its lusts, its hatreds, its envies'.[4] Auden hated the idea of anyone writing his biography, because he did not want his art compromised by association with the foul rag and bone shop of his own life. The mean origins of a work of art should never be allowed to detract from its value, he believed, and I think he was right.

For many years 'Religion' has been going through a similar crisis of authority over its origins. Scholars have started asking: where does religion's menagerie of circus animals come from? The original answer was that it came from the divine or celestial domain, the result of God's prompting or 'Revelation'. In some religions that work of revelation was believed to flow from the direct dictation of God, so that humans were held to be little more than stenographers or neutral conduits for divine inspiration. A weaker version of this claim acknowledged that, given the fallibility of the human mind, it was likely that the 'Divine Dictation' got altered in translation at our end of the transaction, so we should approach religion's claims with our critical faculties keenly alert. The main difficulty faced by the divine dictation model of religion, in either its strong or weak form, is that the manual of ethics that came with it was premised on a stage of human culture that is radically at variance with some of the best values of society today. That is why religion in its more traditional forms finds itself in a state of opposition to some of the moral imperatives of our own time, such as the emancipation of women or the recognition of the rights of sexual minorities; religion is basing its morality on 2,000-year-old values.

This collision between traditional and contemporary values has helped to prompt another interpretation of religion, one that is close to Yeats's re-interpretation of the source of his art. According to this interpretation, religion, like art, should be understood as an entirely human creation. It is a work of the imagination that flows, not from some celestial domain but from the foul rag and bone shop of our own hearts. This understanding of religion need not reduce its value, any more than Yeats's acknowledgement of the lowly source of his poetry diminishes its worth to us. It does mean, however, that we will value it in a different way and for different reasons. It means that we will be less interested in the authority of its origins than in the gifts of interpretation it offers us for understanding our own lives. Lewis Hyde captured this mysterious commerce in his book, *The Gift: How the Creative Spirit Transforms the World*. This is how he describes the transaction between us and the artist:

> A work of art that enters us to feed the soul offers to initiate in us the process of the gifted self which some antecedent gift initiated in the poet. Reading the work, *we* feel gifted for a while, and to the degree that we are able, we respond by creating new work (not art, perhaps, but with the artist's work at hand we suddenly find we can make sense of our own experience). The greatest art offers us images by which to imagine our lives. And once the imagination has been awakened, it is procreative: through it we can give more than we were given, say more than we had to say. This is one reason we cannot read an artist's work by his life. We learn something when we read the life, of course, but the true artist leaves us with the uncanny sense that the experience fails to explain the creation.[5]

The uncanny sense that the experience or humanity of artists fails to explain the astonishing creations that come through them applies to religion as well. We know enough about the origins of religion and its cruel history to be wary of it, maybe even revolted by it; but we also have to acknowledge that, from that seething refuse heap, some wonderful blossoms have bloomed — justice and mercy, love and forgiveness, as well as a whole gallery of tropes and metaphors that have helped us make sense of our lives. Religion at its best is aware of the fragility and ambiguity of the human mediators who are called to act as its conduits of grace to the world. Broken, flawed, unworthy humans are still able to mediate grace to their fellows. 'He saved others, himself he cannot save,'[6] was what the mob chanted at Jesus on the cross, and that is not infrequently the dilemma of the artist as well as the priest. Mediators of grace and meaning to others, their own lives are often characterised by turbulence and tumult. It is certainly the case that some of the most creative priests and artists are well aware that they belong to a covenant of the wounded. Tennessee Williams said he was afraid to exorcise his demons in case he lost his angels. In his prologue to *Cat on a Hot Tin Roof* he developed the idea:

> Of course, it is a pity that so much of all creative work is so closely related to the personality of the one who does it. It is sad and embarrassing and unattractive that those emotions that stir him deeply enough to demand expression, and to charge that expression with some measure of light and power, are nearly all rooted, however changed in their surface, in the particular and sometimes peculiar concerns of the artist himself, that special world, the passions and images of it that each of us weaves about him from birth to death, a web of monstrous complexity, spun forth at a speed that is incalculable to a length beyond measure, from the spider mouth of his own singular perceptions . . . Personal

lyricism is the outcry of prisoner to prisoner from the cell in solitary where each is confined for the duration of his life.[7]

A good example of what he means is found in his play, *The Night of the Iguana*, which exemplifies that cry of prisoner to prisoner that often lies behind the creative act. It comes in Act 3: Shannon, the disgraced Episcopal minister, is quizzing Hannah about her love life. She tells him there had only been two incidents, the first a brief encounter in a cinema when she was sixteen, when a young man had sat down beside her and pushed his knees against hers. The second had been only a couple of years ago. A middle-aged Australian ladies' underwear salesman had paid generously for one of her watercolours. Later that evening he had invited her out on a sampan and, because of his earlier generosity, she accepted. This is how the scene continues:

Hannah: . . . I noticed that he became more and more . . .
Shannon: What?
H: Well . . . *agitated* . . . as the afterglow of the sunset faded out on the water. [*She laughs with delicate sadness.*] Well, finally, eventually, he leaned towards me . . . we were vis-à-vis in the sampan . . . and he looked intensely, passionately into my eyes. [*She laughs again.*] And he said to me: 'Miss Jelkes? Will you do me a favour? Will you do something for me?' 'What?' said I. 'Well,' said he, 'if I turn my back, if I look the other way, will you take off

some piece of your clothes and let me hold it, just hold it?' Then he said, 'It will just take a few seconds.' 'Just a few seconds for what?' I asked him. [*She gives the same laugh again.*] He didn't say for what, but . . .

S: His satisfaction?

H: Yes.

S: That, that . . . sad, dirty little episode, you call it a . . .?

H: [*cutting in sharply*]: Sad it certainly was – for the odd little man – but why do you call it 'dirty'?

S: You mean it didn't disgust you?

H: Nothing human disgusts me unless it's unkind, violent. And I told you how gentle he was . . . apologetic, shy, and really very, well, *delicate* about it.[8]

'Nothing human disgusts me unless it's unkind, violent.' The bleakness in Tennessee Williams's plays is lit with little acts of wistful understanding and forgiving kindness like that, encounters he describes in the same play as, 'broken gates between people so they can reach each other, even if it's just for one night only'.[9] A few moments before she'd described her encounter with the Australian fetishist, Hannah had been trying to reach out over their broken gates to the troubled Shannon. She told him she respected a person like him, 'who had to fight and howl . . . for his decency and his bit of goodness, much more than I respect the lucky ones that just had theirs handed out to them at birth and never afterwards snatched from them by unbearable torments'.[10]

WHERE ALL THE LADDERS START

The 'unbearable torment' in the lives of great artists is sometimes transmuted into a sweeping compassion for the human condition. Though this does not account for what Hyde describes as the artists' 'antecedent gift' for making great art, it certainly informs and infuses it. That is why it is legitimate to see Williams's compassion for the haunted losers in his plays as the fruit of his own unbearable torments. If you'd exorcised his demons, you would have destroyed his angels. The same is true in the moral life. Moral failure can be the mother of compassion, success the father of arrogance. It is no accident that the people in the gospels who understood Jesus's anger at the cruelty of the righteous were sinners tormented by their own unexorcisable demons. Anxious editors came along later and added their own moralistic gloss to the anarchic compassion of Jesus, by informing us that the sinners who were drawn to him all cleaned up their acts and became respectable. I suspect that the opposite is the case and that the people who really understood Jesus were not those who were loved out of their sins but those who knew they were loved *in* them, loved, indeed, because *of* them. That's probably why the French poet Charles Péguy said no one understood Christianity better than the sinner, no one, unless it was the saint. Given the affinity between religion and art, it is not surprising that they have had such a tumultuous relationship.

Religions can be divided into those that reject images and those that affirm them, a conflict that goes back a long way. The rejection of images in Hebrew religion is related to their mistrust of all attempts to explain or find natural equivalents for God, which is not unlike the resistance of artists to explanations of their work. Only God was God, so any representation of God, including verbal representation, came close to idolatry, which is the sin of according absolute value to the contingent or created. This fierce protectiveness of the otherness of God, and refusal to allow the possibility of ever finding an adequate way to express the inexpressibility of the divine mystery, comes close to atheism. Indeed, you get a strong sense from the Hebrew tradition that it would prefer atheists to idolaters, because it was better to deny the existence of God altogether than to identify God with any contingent reality, whether physical or conceptual. This kind of radical theism has a wise mistrust of all religions. It is because religion is a human construct, our response to the possibility of God, that it is in constant danger of falling into the trap Aaron stepped into when he gave the children of Israel the kind of representation of God they longed for – a golden calf, something they could see and touch. That said, the really insidious idols are the conceptual or ideological ones. They have always abounded in religion, and they still multiply today.

It is no accident that the religions that best exemplify the rejection of images had their origin in the desert. The austerity of the wilderness speaks to some people of the otherness of God, unmodified by human interpretation. 'Image-Rejecters' like their religion stripped of everything that might impede the soul's naked encounter with the Divine. A few years ago, I went to Geneva to make a television programme about the great Protestant reformer John Knox, who had spent some of his happiest years in that city, as a friend and disciple of John Calvin. We filmed in the great medieval cathedral, which had once been bright with the colour of imagery and heavy with the smoke of incense. Calvin stripped it bare, and bare it remains, a desert of stone, from which everything has been removed that might distract attention from the utter otherness of God. As someone who prefers religions that let the transcendent filter through the windows of the senses, its fierce and uncompromising emptiness made me shiver, but I was impressed by its audacity.

If rejecters say 'NO' to the claim that the artefacts of human culture can mediate the Divine, the other archetypical response says an equally passionate 'YES'. I contend that the best definition of culture is any widespread behaviour that is transmitted by learning rather than acquired by inheritance. On the basis of that definition, culture is the most distinctly human thing about us. We have many things in common with the other animals with whom we share the planet, but what is most distinctive about us is our creative response to the world. As well as feeding, sheltering and propagating ourselves, we have built cities, composed symphonies, painted pictures, written novels and plays, invented science and philosophy, founded complex civilisations – and developed religions that sought to express the mystery of humanity's struggle to understand its own existence and the universe in which it finds itself. Is human culture, therefore, a rival or an ally of God? Does the lure and fascination of art, science and philosophy draw the soul away from God, or is human culture best interpreted as having itself been inspired by God?

Roman Catholicism is probably the most complete form of a religion that says YES to the mediatorial possibility of imagery, which is why it has been described as 'Baptised Paganism'. Catholicism co-opted the ancient instinct for identifying God with or locating God within the natural order, and claimed it for Christ. It pulled culture close and harnessed it for the service of the Church. If, as one line of recent thought suggests, religion is an entirely human construct, then this ancient controversy must reflect a tension in humanity itself. It is definitely present in Christianity, but we also find it in Islam. The Polish journalist Ryszard Kapuscinski calls it the conflict between the desert and the sea. He said the tension was encapsulated in the city of Algiers, with its open-minded Islam that looks to the Mediterranean; while behind it, in the Atlas Mountains, Islam looks to the desert and the desert dweller's contempt for the genial corruptions of those who live by the sea. We find the same tension in classical Greek thought, described by Nietzsche as the tension between the Dionysian and the Apollonian, the ecstasy of the senses versus controlled rationality. But I want to think now about the Scottish dimension to this ancient quarrel.

I have already mentioned John Knox's sojourn in Geneva. He came back to Scotland in 1559, and in May of that year he preached at the Church of St John in Perth. The congregation responded to his sermon by destroying the beautiful iconography of the church, its shrines and statues and flickering lights. By the following year the Reformation had triumphed in Scotland and it swept away every vestige of what Philip Larkin called the 'vast, moth-eaten musical brocade' of medieval Catholicism. With it went much of the colour, song and closeness to nature that was inherited from the old paganism, and which had been tactfully baptised into Christianity by Catholicism. With it also went Catholicism's rueful tolerance of human weakness, and its genial and not-so genial corruptions. The easy-going 'Yes' of Catholicism had been replaced by the ardent 'No' of radical Protestantism, and it branded Scotland with a particular kind of character, the residue of which still lingers on. This is the beginning of Edwin Muir's romantic lament for what was lost, from his poem 'Scotland 1941':

> A simple sky roofed in that rustic day,
> The busy corn-fields and the haunted holms,
> The green road winding up the ferny brae.
> But Knox and Melville clapped their preaching palms
> And bundled all the harvesters away,
> Hoodicrow Peden in the blighted corn
> Hacked with his rusty beak the starving haulms.
> Out of that desolation we were born.[11]

George Mackay Brown, a convert to Catholicism, was just as trenchant when he described Scotland as 'the Knox-ruined nation'.[12] Whether we agree with it or not, we have to acknowledge that the Reformation left an enduring mark on our national life. Here is a poem by Iain Crichton Smith that could probably not have been written anywhere else. It is called 'Old Woman':

ON REFLECTION

Your thorned back
heavily under the creel
you steadily stamped the rising daffodil.

Your set mouth
forgives no-one, not even God's justice
perpetually drowning law with grace.

Your cold eyes
watched your drunken husband come
unsteadily from Sodom home.

Your grained hands
dandled full and sinful cradles.
You built for your children stone walls.

Your yellow hair
burned slowly in a scarf of grey
wildly falling like the mountain spray.

Finally you're alone
among the unforgiving brass,
the slow silences, the sinful glass.

Who never learned
not even ageing, to forgive
our poor journey and our common grave

while the free daffodils
wave in the valleys and on the hills
the deer look down with their instinctive skills,

and the huge sea
in which your brothers drowned sings slow
over the headland and the peevish crow.[13]

'Who never learned to forgive our poor journey and our common grave.' Religions of the 'No' can breed a flinty and enduring courage like that; and maybe it was a creed suited to those who had to live by the huge sea in which their brothers drowned; but it does tighten the heart with sorrow for the lives of such constricted and unpitying souls. In another of his poems, Crichton Smith told us that, 'From our own weakness only are we kind.'[14] Sadly, sometimes unforgiving religion can turn human weakness into hate.

An interesting paradox is emerging here. We have listened to the work of artists from this piece of the planet, so the claim that Scotland since the Reformation has been an artistically blighted land – a Knox-ruined nation – does not quite stand up. The point I'm coming to is that literature has been Scotland's particular glory for centuries; and its ascendance is directly related to that same blighting Reformation. The reformers exalted literacy and built a school in every parish, so that people could learn to read the Bible. But once people know how to read and write, no tyranny – whether spiritual or political – can contain them forever. A profound literary culture began to flourish in Scotland after the Reformation, subverting authority and challenging hypocrisy. That is why the historian T.C. Smout says that 'the peculiar richness in the flowering of the Scottish cultural enlightenment after 1740 can be partly explained by a process of action and reaction from the

Reformation.'[15] We might have pulled down the altars and images, but we became a literate, argumentative nation that exalted words – and still does. Scotland is full of writers, published and unpublished. And this is the point: there is something about writing that mirrors the great controversy over images, the dispute between those who said 'YES' to them and those who said 'NO'. In *The Unquiet Grave* Cyril Connolly captured the duality:

> There are two ways to be a great writer. One way is like Homer, Shakespeare and Goethe to accept life completely, the other (Pascal's, Proust's, Leopardi's, Baudelaire's) is to refuse ever to lose sight of its horror.[16]

The YES! and the NO! Both religion and art stand astonished before the being of being, the there-ness, this-ness, that-ness of things, and they respond with both wonder and horror. Heidegger said art was not imitation or representation of the real – it was the more real.[17] The artist's concentrated seeing heightens and enlarges the there-ness of things. Yes, and the strangeness of things. 'Rilke said of Cezanne that he did not paint, "I like it", he painted, "There it is".'[18] In contrast to art, which is content to paint or write or transpose the there-ness of things, religion has a fatal need to explain them and tell us precisely how they came to be. But if you abandon religion's explanatory function, you can sometimes get it back as an art that refuses ever to lose sight of life's horror, in Cyril Connolly's phrase. Behind the architecture of religious doctrine in its pessimistic mode can be heard a denunciatory 'NO' to the crimes and follies of humanity.

Recognising what flawed, struggling creatures we are, we can reach out to each other over broken gates and remind ourselves, as Iain Crichton Smith put it, that 'from our own weakness only are we kind'.[19] We need both forms of religious and artistic honesty, the 'YES' and the 'NO'; but I believe we are in greater need of the 'YES' today. I have no reason to suppose that individuals are less forgiving than they ever were, less disposed to reach out to others over broken gates, but there is something ugly and unforgiving about our common culture at the moment, reflected in the gleeful vindictiveness of social media and bullying newspapers. That is why I am proud that it was a melancholy Scottish poet who told us it was 'from our own weakness only are we kind' and went on to remind us that it is never too late 'to forgive our poor journey and our common grave'.[20]

4

AUDEN: THE POET PREACHER

I quoted the great English poet W.H. Auden on the great Irish poet William Butler Yeats in the previous chapter, but I want to turn to Auden again and focus on him exclusively in this essay. He was born in York in 1907. When he died in 1973 he was reckoned to be one of the great literary figures of the twentieth century. Twenty years after his death he got a second fifteen minutes of fame from the 1994 film *Four Weddings and a Funeral,* in which John Hannah recited one of Auden's poems, 'Stop All the Clocks', at the funeral of his character's partner, which begins:

> Stop all the clocks, cut off the telephone,
> Prevent the dog from barking with a juicy bone,
> Silence the pianos and with muffled drum
> Bring out the coffin, let the mourners come.[1]

Auden spent most of his adult life in New York City, retiring to England in 1972, a sad and dishevelled figure who chain-smoked constantly, had a face like a dried-up riverbed and always wore carpet slippers, even on intercontinental flights.

AUDEN: THE POET PREACHER

T.S. Eliot complained that Auden tired him by explaining things and preaching at him. His years as a teacher certainly gave Auden a didactic style, but the accusation of preaching is probably a more perceptive criticism. Auden said of himself that he colonised rather than explored modern verse. Colonisers are people who exploit people and places for their own ends. And Auden's purpose seems to have been a desire to express certain theological themes that became important to him after his return to Christianity. He explained his return in a letter.

> One fine summer night in June 1933 I was sitting on a lawn after dinner with three colleagues, two women and one man. We were talking casually about every day matters when, quite suddenly and unexpectedly, something happened. I felt myself invaded by a power which, though I consented to it, was irresistible and certainly not mine. For the first time in my life I knew exactly what it means to love one's neighbour as oneself. Among the various factors which several years later brought me back to the Christian faith in which I had been brought up, the memory of this experience and asking myself what it could mean was one of the most crucial, though, at the time it occurred, I thought I had done with Christianity for good.[2]

In one of his most famous poems, 'In Memory of W.B. Yeats', which I quoted in the previous essay, Auden said that 'poetry makes nothing happen: it survives in the valley of its making'. While I don't think Auden contradicted himself by writing poetry intended to make something happen, I do think his faith profoundly influenced what he wrote, and it might even be said that he came close to using his verse as an exploration of Christian theology.

Two Christian doctrines preoccupied him. The first was the Incarnation. This is sometimes expressed as the claim that Jesus was God disguised as a man, 'the Word made Flesh', as John's Gospel puts it. Its other, subtler meaning is that the divine is no longer to be found in some transcendent realm but is to be found among ordinary people doing ordinary things. The 'Great Presences' are no longer discovered in lofty events with spotlights and soaring orchestras, they now come softly among us as life goes on around us. Behind this idea are the great Christian inversions: the maker of all things, born in a stable; the divine son, casually executed near a garbage dump outside the city. His other preoccupation was the problem of suffering: if there is no God and no ultimate meaning to things, then suffering is just a grim fact among other grim facts. But if there is a God, an allegedly loving God, then suffering becomes a theological problem: how does God justify it and allow it to continue for one minute longer? A not very convincing way round the problem is to assert that God suffers alongside us in the world, and feels the pain of every sparrow's fall, but that is the price we pay for the freedom of the human will.

> Are not two sparrows sold for a farthing? And one of them shall not fall to the ground without your father.
> — Matthew, 10:29

The sparrow's fall is a major problem for Christian theology, mainly because it thinks it has an explanation for everything, and the explanation it reaches for here, human freedom, does not help – unless you are completely indifferent to the suffering of the other animals we share the planet with. The usual explanation for suffering is that God has given us freedom of the will, which includes the freedom to make wrong choices, and it is our wrong choices that cause the pain that infuses human history. Well, there may be something in that, as far as humans are concerned, but how does it justify the fall of sparrows? I suspect it is the case that for centuries Christian theology was indifferent to the suffering of animals and didn't see it as a problem: after all, they were created for our benefit and to serve our needs. Well, that may justify the lethal shock that kills them in the abattoir but, as the English mystic Evelyn Underhill once exclaimed: 'What about cancer in fish?'

Auden brought some of these ideas into his poem 'Friday's Child'. Behind it also lay the thought of the German theologian martyred by the Nazis, Dietrich Bonhoeffer, who claimed that modern man had come of age, and now had to live without the old consolations of belief, and that includes the explanations that do not explain.

> Our coming of age leads us to a true recognition of our situation before God. God would have us know that we must live as men who manage our lives without him. The God who is with us is the God who forsakes us. The God who lets us live in the world without the

working hypothesis of God is the God before whom we stand continually. Before God and with God we live without God.³

And part of that coming of age, according to Auden, involves the rejection of the possibility of God.

> Since the analogies are rot
> Our senses based belief upon,
> We have no means of learning what
> Is going on,
>
> And must put up with having learned
> All proofs or disproofs that we tender
> Of his existence are returned
> Unopened to the sender.⁴

There is more than a hint of the death of God in Auden's homage to another of his heroes, 'In Memory of Sigmund Freud'. Describing how Freud had changed our world for ever, he wrote of his critics:

> Of course they called on God, but he went his way
> down among the lost people like Dante, down
> to the stinking fosse where the injured
> lead the ugly life of the rejected,
>
> and showed us what evil is, not, as we thought,
> deeds that must be punished, but our lack of faith,
> our dishonest mood of denial,
> the concupiscence of the oppressor.⁵

AUDEN: THE POET PREACHER

Yes, Auden was a preacher, and, like all good preachers, he preached mainly to himself, but we now know that Auden not only preached at us, he practised what he preached, with many secret acts of caring that were only revealed after his death, such as the one described by Alan Bennett in an entry in his *Diaries* for 27 March 2014.

> ... a good piece on Auden by Edward Mendelson the NYRB. I buy a copy and it is a revelation detailing some of Auden's almost obsessively secretive charities – two orphans to be supported all his life, the support transferred to a further two once a pair had grown up; kicking up a fuss over the prompt payment of a cheque from a publisher, the reason only becoming clear when the cheque was endorsed after payment showing it had gone towards keeping a shelter for the homeless that would otherwise have closed. It's the kind of goodness one might meet in a Victorian novel and not, I think, figuring in any of Auden's various biographies and memoirs. Scrupulously secretive I suppose he was lest the motive for his charities were sullied by any hint of self-advertisement.[6]

Eliot was right, W.H. Auden was a preacher all right – and a good one!

5

THE CALEDONIAN ANTISYZYGY

The word 'antisyzygy' was coined by G. Gregory Smith in his book published in 1919, *Scottish Literature: Character and Influence*, to define the oppositional polarities in the Scottish character, but it got its second wind from Hugh MacDiarmid in his book *Scottish Eccentrics*, published in 1936, where he talked about 'the Caledonian Antisyzygy' or '. . . the contradictions of character . . . the antinomies and antithetical impulses . . . that are in the makeup of almost every distinguished Scot'. Since then, the Caledonian Antisyzygy – or the presence of duelling polarities within the Scottish soul – has become something of a national cliché.

Though I want to explore its Scottish expression in this essay, it is far from unique to Scotland. It is a human characteristic expressed in many different ways. As already mentioned, Nietzsche discovered it in classical Greek thought, when he talked about the tension between the Dionysian and the Apollonian, the hot ecstasy of the sensual life versus the cool control of the rational life. It is present in English history in the conflict between Cavalier and Roundhead or Hedonist and Puritan, represented in Shakespeare's *Twelfth Night* in the conflict between Sir Toby Belch and Malvolio: 'Dost thou think because thou art virtuous there will be no more cakes and ale?'[1]

Since religious thinkers trace everything back to the guiding hand of God, it was inevitable that in the compulsions of human behaviour they saw God at work. In Christian theology, its classic duality is probably best expressed by Saint Paul in his Letter to the Romans:

> I do not understand my own actions. For I do not do what I want, but I do the very thing I hate. Now if I do what I do not want, I agree that the law is good. So then it is no longer I that do it, but sin which dwells within me . . . I can will what is right, but I cannot do it. For I do not do the good I want, but the evil I do not want is what I do. Now if I do what I do not want, it is no longer I that do it, but sin which dwells within me.
>
> — Romans, 7:15–20

He found the resolution to the puzzle of his own behaviour in the mysterious will of God.

> We know that in everything God works for good with those who love him, who are called according to his purpose. For those whom he foreknew he also predestined . . . and those whom he predestined he also called; and those whom he called he also justified . . .
>
> — Romans, 8:28

The word translated 'predestined' here comes from a Greek verb meaning 'to see ahead' or 'preordain', so the sense is that God is in control of human history and everything that happens has already been fixed or predetermined by him, the way a movie in production works to an established script. That is certainly how the influential Swiss reformer John Calvin understood the human situation. He was in no doubt that . . .

> By predestination we mean the eternal decree of God, by which he determined with himself whatever he wished to happen with regard to every man. All are not created on equal terms, but some are preordained to eternal life, others to eternal damnation; and, accordingly, as each has been created for one or other of these ends, we say that he has been predestinated to life or death.[2]

John Knox was never as pitiless a thinker as Calvin, but it was through him that the Predestinationist virus was brought to Scotland, where it became the grimmest of all the forms of the Caledonian Antisyzygy, seen at its fiercest in two great classics of Scottish literature. The most famous is Robert Louis Stevenson's novel, *The Strange Case of Dr Jekyll and Mr Hyde*, which is as much about the split personality of nineteenth-century Edinburgh as it is about the good Dr Jekyll and his evil other self, Mr Hyde.

But there is an earlier and greater Scottish novel that covers the same territory with more profundity and chilling calmness of purpose. *The Private Memoirs and Confessions of a Justified Sinner* is the masterpiece of James Hogg, a self-educated Borders shepherd, whose alleged coarseness and vulgarity were both mocked and misunderstood by the bourgeois literati of Edinburgh society. Hogg, a contemporary of Sir Walter Scott, was born in 1770 and died in 1835. *Confessions* was published in 1824. The 'justified sinner' of Hogg's text is a young Borders aristocrat called Robert Cowan, who comes to believe that he has been predestined by God to eternal salvation, irrespective of how he behaves. As we have already seen, this vocabulary comes to us from Saint Paul in his Letter to the Romans, Chapter 8, which seems to teach that our eternal destination is not determined by how we have acted in this life, but by the preordained will of God before we were even born:

For those whom he foreknew he also predestined . . . and those whom he predestined he also called; and those whom he called he also justified . . .

These convoluted phrases gave rise to the doctrine of Predestination, the idea that, even before they were born, God had chosen some humans for salvation and others for eternal damnation or unending torment, as described by the Irish writer James Joyce in a sermon he heard as a boy:

. . . the sulphurous brimstone which burns in hell is a substance which is specially designed to burn for ever and for ever with unspeakable fury . . . our earthly fire destroys at the same time as it burns . . . but the fire of hell has this property, that it preserves that which it burns, and, though it rages with incredible intensity, it rages for ever.[3]

ON REFLECTION

This doctrine, comforting to those who knew they belonged to the elect, gave rise to a consequent theory, called 'antinomianism', which held that the elect could behave any way they liked on earth, since they had already been inoculated against damnation by the sovereign will of God. It formed a prominent part of Calvinist thinking in Enlightenment Scotland, and Robert Burns captured the whole mad business in 'Holy Willie's Prayer':

> O Thou, wha in the heavens dost dwell,
> Wha, as it pleases best thysel',
> Sends ane to heaven and ten to hell,
>   A' for thy glory,
> And no for ony guid or ill
>   They've done afore thee!
>
> I bless and praise thy matchless might,
> Whan thousands thou hast left in night,
> That I am here afore thy sight,
>   For gifts an' grace,
> A burnin' an' a shinin' light,
>   To a' this place.
>
>   What was I, or my generation,
> That I should get sic exaltation?
> I, wha deserved most just damnation
>   For broken laws
> Sax thousand years ere my creation
>   Thro' Adam's cause.

THE CALEDONIAN ANTISYZYGY

The wonderful thing about being predestined to Heaven by God's grace was that you could not forfeit it by fleshly behaviour, which was just as well, because it turns out that Holy Willie is a lecherous old goat . . .

>But yet – O Lord – confess I must –
>At times I'm fash'd wi' fleshly lust;
>And sometimes too, in warldly trust
>>Vile self gets in;
>But Thou remembers we are dust,
>>Defil'd wi' sin. –
>
>O Lord – yestreen – Thou kens – wi' Meg –
>Thy pardon I sincerely beg!
>O may't ne'er be a living plague,
>>To my dishonour!
>And I'll ne'er lift a lawless leg
>>Again upon her. –
>
>Besides, I farther maun avow,
>Wi' Leezie's lass, three times – I trow –
>But Lord, that Friday I was fou
>>When I cam near her;
>Or else, Thou kens, Thy servant true
>>Wad never steer her. –

> Maybe Thou lets this fleshly thorn
> Buffet thy servant e'en and morn,
> Lest he o'er proud and high should turn,
>   That he's sae gifted;
> If sae, Thy hand maun e'en be borne
>   Until Thou lift it.[4]

How does Burns's cheeky humour relate to Hogg's much grimmer novel? In his introduction to the Canongate edition, David Groves tells us that 'no one will understand very much about Hogg's *Confessions* on first reading'. For a start, the story is told twice, from different perspectives, but there is also a third voice throughout that we ought to listen to, and it is probably Hogg's own. The protagonist is Robert Cowan, the second son of the Laird of Dalcastle. But, since little is obvious in this book, he may actually be the natural son of Robert Wringhim, the local Calvinist minister and an ardent Predestinarian. The first or editor's narrative is a brisk and superficially rational account of Cowan's murderous career and mysterious disappearance. However, doubts are cast on the objectivity of the editor by the arrogant way he relates to the poor working people who appear in the story, whose voice may be expressing Hogg's own attitude to these complex events.

In the second narrative, the 'confessions' proper, we dive straight into the mind of the accused, as he tries to understand and offer an account of the terrible things he fears he may have done. Apart from his cruel rejection by his legal father, the Laird of Dalcastle, two influences have worked on him. The first is his stepfather, the fanatical

THE CALEDONIAN ANTISYZYGY

Robert Wringhim, who steeps him in the obsessive intricacies of predestinationist theology. A key passage in understanding the evolution of the lonely and insecure young man into the confused monster he becomes, follows Mr Wringhim's announcement that he has received assurance from God that his stepson is indeed among the predestined elect:

> From that moment, I conceived it decreed, not that I should be a minister of the gospel, but a champion of it, to cut off the enemies of the Lord from the face of the earth; and I rejoiced in the commission, finding it more congenial to my nature to be cutting sinners off with the sword, than to be haranguing them from the pulpit, striving to produce an effect which God, by his act of absolute predestination, had for ever rendered impracticable. The more I pondered on these things the more I saw of the folly and inconsistency of ministers, in spending their lives striving and remonstrating with sinners in order to induce them to do that which they had it not in their power to do. Seeing that God had from all eternity decided the fate of every individual that was to be born of woman, how vain was it in man to endeavour to save those whom their Maker had, by an unchangeable decree, doomed to destruction. I could not disbelieve the doctrine which the best of men had taught me, and toward which he made the whole of the Scriptures to bear, and yet it made the economy of the Christian world appear to me as an absolute contradiction. How much more wise would it be, thought I, to begin and cut sinners off with the sword![5]

This is where the second influence is brought to bear, through the agency of a mysterious tempter called Gil-Martin, who persuades Robert that God's elect have been liberated from conventional moral restraints in order to perform his cleansing work. Gil-Martin is a Gaelic name for a fox and there is no doubt that Hogg wants us to recognize him as the devil, the great deceiver of humankind, who can appear as an angel of light and instrument of God. Under the twin influences of a deranged religious ideology and satanic seduction, Robert stumbles into his murderous career. But he remains a troubled and suicidal man who kills himself in despair, taking his demonic alter ego with him. The book concludes with another dismissive snort from the editor, who leaves us none the wiser as to whether Gil-Martin ever existed outside Robert Cowan's troubled mind.

It is the third voice in the book, neither the editor's nor Robert Cowan's, that provides us with the clue to Hogg's intentions in writing it. Though *Confessions* is a darkly gothic narrative, it is also very funny, and nowhere funnier than in the account of the great Auchtermuchty preaching. Auchtermuchty, a small town in Perthshire, is gripped by religion:

> There was nought to be heard, neither night nor day, but preaching, praying, argumentation, an' catechising in a' the famous town o' Auchtermuchty. The young men wooed their sweethearts out o' the Song o' Solomon, an' the girls returned answers in strings o' verses out o' the Psalms.' Into this town, one sabbath, strides a stranger 'clothed in a robe of black sackcloth,

THE CALEDONIAN ANTISYZYGY

that flowed all around him, and trailed far behind, and they weened him an angel, come to exhort them, in disguise.[6]

The inhabitants of Auchtermuchty are electrified by the stranger's preaching from a text in Ezekiel:

> I will overturn, overturn, overturn it; and it shall be no more, until he comes, whose right it is, and I will give it him.

From this text he preached

> ... such a sermon as never was heard by human ears, at least never by ears of Auchtermuchty. It was a true, sterling, gospel sermon – it was striking, sublime and awful in the extreme. He finally made out the IT, mentioned in the text, to mean, properly and positively, the notable town of Auchtermuchty. He proved all the people in it, to their perfect satisfaction, to be in the gall of bitterness and the bond of iniquity, and he assured them that God would overturn them, their principles, and professions; and that they should be no more, until the Devil, the town's greatest enemy, came, and then it should be given unto him for a prey, for it was his right, and to him it belonged, if there was not forthwith a radical change made in all their opinions and modes of worship.[7]

The narrator reminds us that, 'Nothing in the world delights a truly religious people so much as consigning them to eternal damnation', so they hang on the preacher's every word. What saves the town from the perdition to which the visitor is leading it is not the sophistication of the local intelligentsia, who are all seduced by his eloquence, but the simple decency of an uneducated old man, Robin Ruthven. When his words of warning against the dark arts of the preacher are scornfully rejected by the town, he persuades them by a simple ruse:

> Robin Ruthven came in amang the thrang [. . .], and, with the greatest readiness and simplicity, just took haud o' the side o' the wide gown, and in sight of a' present, held it aside as high as the preacher's knee, and, behold, there was a pair o' cloven feet! The auld thief was fairly catched in the very height o' his proud conquest, an' put down by an auld carl. He could feign nae mair, but, gnashing on Robin wi' his teeth, he dartit into the air like a fiery dragon, an' keust a reid rainbow o'er the taps o' the Lowmonds.[8]

It is the auld wife of one of the weavers of Auchtermuchty who draws the moral for us:

> . . . whenever you are doubtfu' of a man, take auld Robin Ruthven's plan, an' look for the cloven foot, for it's a thing that winna weel hide; an' it appears whiles where ane wadna think o't. It will keek out frae aneath the parson's gown, the lawyer's wig, and the Cameronian's blue bannet; but still there is a gouden rule whereby to detect it, an' that never, never fails.[9]

THE CALEDONIAN ANTISYZYGY

The predestinationism that Hogg was satirising in his novel imparted to post-Reformation Scottish religion a high level of spiritual anxiety. Were we of the elect or of the damned? Were we destined for Heaven or Hell? That was the form predestinationist anxiety took for people of faith, but I wonder if behind its religious expression it did not leave a lasting imprint on the Scottish psyche. Knox thought there could be no compromise in religion. The soul was faced with a stark choice between God and the Devil, Protestantism or Catholicism. He said there was 'nae middis' or middle way; it had to be one thing or the other. Knox identified the Roman Catholic church as the 'Dangerous Other', the opposing pole against which the Reformed church had to define and understand itself, but in doing so he set a trap Scotland would fall into when it entered the Union of Parliaments with England in 1707.

In the beginning, the Union fortified the idea of Catholicism as the 'other' against which England and Scotland defined themselves as Protestant nations, and it was amplified by our participation in the spread of the British Empire in the late eighteenth century, though our enthusiasm had its ridiculous side. A key event in the consolidation of Scotland's membership of the United Kingdom was the visit to Edinburgh of King George IV in 1822, the whole affair stage-managed by the great impresario himself, Sir Walter Scott. The corpulent monarch wore pink tights under the kilt he had been persuaded to wear for his landing in Leith, where he was met by Scotland's elite, who were also wrapped in tartan, the very tartan that had been proscribed after the battle of Culloden on 16 April 1746 had ended the romantic attempt by the Highland clans to re-establish the Stuart monarchy in Scotland. Tartan, banned after that famous defeat, was now the official dress of the Highland regiments that were the shock-troops of the British Empire, of which the stout Hanoverian monarch was now the primary symbol. Walter Scott knew an antisyzygy when he saw one. A firm supporter of the Union, he wrapped Protestant Scotland in the very plaid that had been the badge of Catholic opposition to the House of Hanover, whose representative he was now welcoming to his northern kingdom.

Another paradox is that the British Empire that had reinforced Scotland's hatred of Catholicism as the demonic other was the same force that brought Catholicism back into its midst, when Ireland became part of the Union in 1801. Scotland had spent centuries turning itself into a Protestant fortress, so when the potato famine of the nineteenth century forced thousands of Irish Catholics to come to Scotland in search of a better life, they were harshly rejected by the Kirk. Panicked by their arrival, the Kirk was outraged when the United Kingdom Government told them that the Irish were citizens of the British Empire and had as much right to settle in Scotland as the Scots had to settle in Ireland.

Things were shifting in Scotland, anyway. The Protestant–Catholic duality was slowly reversing its emphasis, and the time came when the Catholic other became the loudest voice of Christian Scotland. A pivotal moment was the death of the Catholic Archbishop of Glasgow, Cardinal Thomas Winning, in June 2001. By the time of his death, the consensus was that he had become the public face of Christianity in Scotland, where the Catholic church was now numerically as strong as the Kirk that had so bitterly campaigned against its return to Scotland in the nineteenth century. A number of factors had contributed to this dramatic turning of the tables. Let me suggest three.

After the Union of Parliaments of 1707 removed Scotland's seat of government to London, the annual meeting of the General Assembly of the Church of Scotland in Edinburgh had been the closest we had to our own parliament; but with the coming of devolution in 1999 and the restoration of some elements of political autonomy to the reconstituted Scottish Parliament, the significance of the General Assembly declined, and attention shifted from the Kirk's Assembly Rooms at the top of the Royal Mile to the Holyrood Parliament at the bottom.

Another factor was the insatiable need of modern news media, which had become a dominant factor in the digitised, interconnected world we now lived in. The Church of Scotland is a non-hierarchical organisation. It elects Moderators of the General Assembly as its figure-head, but – having a healthy suspicion of the dangers of power and prominence – it removes them from office after a year. So where does the hungry media go when it wants an instant comment on the issues of the day, especially if they are about the tensions between religion and the emerging secular ethic of Scotland? Cardinals and archbishops are the obvious go-to people. As authority figures who possess real power, they can speak for the whole Church. Cardinal Winning obliged by speaking trenchantly against the spirit of the age, with its secularising agenda of gay rights and other abominations, whereas no single individual could speak for the Kirk; and when the Kirk did speak at its annual assembly in Edinburgh, it rarely spoke with a single voice, argument and disagreement being part of its essence.

The third factor was the increasing dominance of secular thinking in Scotland. This was partly related to the general decline of religious belief throughout Europe in the twentieth century, but its more positive aspect was the increasing confidence of thinkers who derived their ethics not from religious tradition but from humanity's own reflections on the best way to order its life. In the twentieth century this moral revolution had two significant pressure points. The more important was the movement for the liberation of women from male dominance that began with the campaign that won them the vote in 1918, though full equality with men in society is still a distant goal. The Feminist movement caused particular problems for religious institutions that based their ethics on the norms of patriarchal societies from the distant past, not the progressive values of modern democracies. The Church of Scotland was one of the earliest faith communities to come to terms with the Feminist revolution. It ordained its first woman minister in 1969, to be followed, a quarter of a century later, in 1994, by the Church of England and the Scottish Episcopal Church. Female ordination is not yet under serious discussion in the Roman Catholic church, one of the mightiest institutions on earth. Its size probably has a lot to do with its resistance to change, small ships finding it easier to navigate changes of direction than mighty ocean liners.

But debate over the status of women was nothing

THE CALEDONIAN ANTISYZYGY

compared to religious anger at the prospect of emancipating gay people in Church and society. The loudest voice against both of these liberalising trends was Cardinal Winning's, so we observed the fascinating reversal of the once-despised Catholic other assuming the moralistic mantle of Calvinist Scotland, and with the same Knoxian tone. 'Nae middis!' 'No compromise!' Another swerve of the Caledonian antisyzygy! But the whirligig of time kept spinning and it soon brought in its revenges, as Shakespeare reminds us in *Twelfth Night*.[10]

In 2003, following the death of Cardinal Winning, Keith Patrick O'Brien, Archbishop of St Andrews and Edinburgh, was appointed by the Pope as the Scottish cardinal. O'Brien had been a closet liberal who had found Winning's tone harsh and unsympathetic in the debates of the time. But when he came back from Rome with his red hat, he was under strict orders from the Pope to maintain the Catholic church's opposition to the secularising agenda that was sweeping Scotland. He did what he was told, and he became even more vehement, more Knoxian, than Winning. His tragedy was that he was himself a gay man, and the latest struggle of the antisyzygy was fought out within his own soul. When his sexual history was finally exposed, he resigned in disgrace in 2013, and a hush descended on the battlefield. The angry voices muted. The religious conflict quietened as if ashamed of the tragedy it had wrought. And on his death in 2018 there was an outpouring of sympathy for the disgraced cardinal.

This is a history that leaves us with some important questions. Can humans find a way of dealing with the divisions and polarities that are an abiding part of their character, without splitting into warring camps that hate each other? The perfect religion, the perfect political system, can never exist, because it would take perfect humans to contrive them, and perfect humans have never been born. But, oh, the hunger we have for them! The lust for the perfect, the complete! Think of the injuries we have done to one another in our vain search for those unrealisable perfections. It is time to remember that it is from our own weakness, not our strength, that we learn to be kind, as the old Hebridean poet taught us. The dualities of the Caledonian antisyzygy may, after all, be the best guide to wise living.

6

AT REQUIEM MASS IN THE USHER HALL

The human being is a dying animal. So are all the other animals on the planet, you might reply. You are correct, so let me amend my opening statement: we are the only animal that *knows* it will die and it is that knowledge that defines us. The other animals, certainly the more advanced ones, seem to *mourn* the death of their fellows and are touched by their loss; but I do not think they live their lives with the knowledge that one day they too will die, the way we do. This fact points to the gigantic difference between us and them, a difference that makes us not only the most intelligent, but the most tragic of animals. We have achieved a level of self-consciousness and understanding that makes us an object of interest to ourselves. Unlike the other creatures who act without thought in an instinctive way, *we are conscious of how we act and watch ourselves doing so*. That is why in Hamlet, Shakespeare warned us that human resolution 'is sicklied o'er with the pale cast of thought'. One of the things we think about is death. We are a dying animal, and we know it. The philosopher Martin Heidegger described us as *beings towards death*,[1] death defining our life the way a frame defines a painting, or the silence at the end of a piece of music completes its meaning. A sentence is not finished till it has a full stop, called a period, and our lives need a dying to finish or complete them. Though we understand with our minds that a world without death would be a world accursed, we hate death anyway, because of the way, in a fraction of a second, it can take out of the world a life that is precious to us, a life on which we so depend that when it goes our heart goes with it.

> Never again, no matter how long I look out of the window, will I see your tall thin figure walking across the park past the dwarf pine past the stumps, and then climb the ha-ha and come across the lawn. Our jokes have gone for ever.[2]

Those words come from the diary of the painter Dora Carrington, written just before she killed herself, knowing she could no longer live in a world that did not contain the presence of her friend Lytton Strachey.

Many scholars think it is our outrage at death, our refusal to believe in the absolute annihilation of those we love, that lies at the root of religion. Of the religions that deny the ultimate victory of death over the human soul, Christianity is probably the most defiant and eloquent on the subject. And within Christianity, the most advanced thanatology is found within the Roman Catholic tradition, reaching its height of beauty and wistfulness in the Solemn Requiem or Mass for the Departed.

The Requiem is a special version of the Mass, with subtle shifts of emphasis and tone, and it is usually celebrated

AT REQUIEM MASS IN THE USHER HALL

in the presence of the corpse, for whom it is a cry for mercy to God. Before recent liturgical changes in the Catholic church brightened things up and took a lot of the anguish out of funerals, a requiem was more sombre than the normal mass. The colour of the vestments was black and instead of the usual creamy-coloured beeswax candles, the candles used were an unbleached dark orange in colour. The more explosive notes of joy from the mass were removed, such as the *Gloria in Excelsis Deo* or Glory to God in the Highest, the joyful canticle that usually begins the mass. And there were subtle changes to the *Agnus Dei* before Communion: *Grant them rest,* instead of *Have mercy upon us.*

But the most tremendous addition to the traditional liturgy of the Solemn Requiem Mass was the great hymn or sequence, the *Dies Irae*, a dramatic meditation on judgement after death. The fear of judgement and damnation after death hung over medieval Christian thought like a funeral pall, and the *Dies Irae* was its most anguished cry:

> Day of wrath and doom impending,
> David's word with Sybil's blending!
> Heaven and earth in ashes ending.
> O what fear man's bosom rendeth,
> When from heav'n the Judge descendeth,
> On whose sentence all dependeth.
>
> What shall I, frail man, be pleading?
> Who for me be interceding,
> When the just are mercy needing?

ON REFLECTION

Lo! The book exactly worded,
Wherein all hath been recorded;
Thence shall judgement be awarded.

When the judge his seat attaineth,
And each hidden deed arraigneth,
Nothing unavenged remaineth.

Ah! That day of tears and mourning!
From the dust of earth returning,
Man for judgement must prepare him:
Spare, O God, in mercy spare him.[3]

This is the note in the Requiem that can still send a shiver down our spines, even if we no longer believe in the Final Judgement it proclaims. Death still summons us to thought and reflection about our lives, but in today's secular culture the only solemn requiem we are ever likely to attend will be in our local concert hall to listen to Mozart's meditation on the one fact that unites and defines us all: our dying. But is Mozart's Requiem now just a concert piece, something we sit in comfortable seats listening to, as we suck complacently on our peppermints? Or can it also be used to prompt reflection on final things, remembering that, while the day of our death may no longer be a day of wrath and doom, it will, nevertheless, be the end of us?

It is up to us, of course, but it seems a pity to use these occasions only for aesthetic enjoyment. But how do we use a concert performance of the requiem for reflection as well as pleasure? Obviously, by *attending,* by leaning into the meaning behind the words and music. We are brought

AT REQUIEM MASS IN THE USHER HALL

here to a threshold that prompts serious reflection about death and how to prepare for it. Think of the sorrow of letting someone close to you die unforgiven, because they hurt you in the past and you die still bearing the grudge. Just as sad is to let your love and appreciation go unsaid because you never got round to it. Do it now. Pick up the phone. Remember Bernard O'Donoghue's poem 'Going Without Saying':

> It is a great pity we don't know
> When the dead are going to die
> So that, over a last companionable
> Drink, we could tell them
> How much we liked them.
> Happy the man who, dying, can
> Place his hand on his heart and say:
> At least I didn't neglect to tell
> The thrush how beautifully she sings.[4]

And think how the journey towards the grave accelerates as you get older, so look around in wonder as it speeds towards its end. 'Look thy last on all things lovely every day,' said Walter de la Mare. Be grateful not only to life, but to death as well, for without it, life would be robbed of its purpose and intensity. An infinity of postponement would have removed the need to work while it was yet day, since no night would ever come to bring it to an end. Imagine the infinite boredom of a deathless universe! We should be grateful to death for delivering us from that purposeless endlessness. But we should also yield to the sorrow of all that dying, all that going from us, all those empty chairs, all those phone numbers that no longer connect to a beloved voice. All of this is gathered into this solemn and beautiful hour. Yes, it is more than a concert; it is death's gift to us – the dying animal.

7

THOSE FALLEN LADDERS AGAIN

I want to begin this essay by going back to the poetry of William Butler Yeats. A recent biography claims that many of his inspirations came from the occult. Yeats was 51 when he married Georgie Hyde-Lees on 20 October 1917, and his new wife was only 21. It was a complex relationship, and there is evidence that Yeats was in love with someone else at the time. What cemented the relationship, at any rate during its early years, was his new wife's facility for automatic or ghost writing, allegedly at the dictation of the dead. Brenda Maddox, author of *Yeats's Ghosts*, suggests that his young wife used the facility not only to capture her husband's interest, but to direct their sexual relationship. But George's ghosts provided more than sexual encouragement and advice on domestic arrangements; they also provided powerful images that went into some of Yeats's most famous poems, once he'd come to accept that 'the foul rag and bone shop' of his heart was the real source of his inspiration, not some exalted sphere beyond himself.

Something similar has happened to many of us in the Christian Church. Our theological ladders have all fallen, so we have to lie down where they all started from anyway – our own hearts. I want to offer some preliminary notes for the work of reconstruction we must all engage in, if inspiration is to return to the Jesus movement, however widely we interpret it. This essay will be in three parts: part one about the mystery we call God; part two about that collection of ancient documents we call the New Testament; and part three will be about the Church itself.

Among contemporary theologians there are three broad approaches to the mystery we call God: *naive-realism, non-realism* and *critical-realism*. Let me explain their differences by reference to the famous passage in the Book of Exodus, where Moses hears God speaking to him from a burning bush and is commissioned to lead the Israelites out of Egypt:

> Now Moses kept the flock of Jethro his father in law, the Priest of Midian: and he led the flock to the backside of the desert, and came to the mountain of God, even to Horeb. And the angel of the Lord appeared to him in a flame of fire out of the midst of a burning bush: and he looked, and, behold, the bush burned with fire, and the bush was not consumed . . . And when the Lord saw that he turned aside to see, God called unto him out of the midst of the bush, and said, Moses, Moses. And he said, Here am I.
>
> – Exodus, 3:1–4

The naive-realist would say of this passage that God had actually entered the bush and had spoken human, recordable words to Moses in his own language. The non-realist would say that what was happening was happening, but it was taking place only in the imagination of Moses. The position of critical-realist Christians is less easy to describe. They believe that there is a 'transcendent other' behind the universe, but that our encounters with it are filtered through and distorted by our own human fallibility. After all, they would say, if we can get the truth of encounters with other humans as badly wrong as we often do, then our encounters with the mystery we call God are bound to be subject to the same mistakes and distortions, which is why all religious claims require careful examination and interpretation. This is how the influential theologian John Hick put it:

> Religious experience occurs in many different forms, and the critical realist interpretation enables us to see how these may nevertheless be different authentic responses to the Real. But they may also not be. They may instead be human self-delusion. Or they may be a mixture of both. And so a critical stance in relation to them is essential.[1]

No matter what position we take on the reality of God, therefore, a difficulty affects them all. There is an old paradox in philosophy called the paradox of appearance: is there a world out there that is independent of our perception of it? Common sense would suggest that there has to be; but the fact remains that we only know it, only get it, through our own perception of it. It is our mind that puts us in touch with what's out there. So, there is a sense in which it is true to say that it is our mind that calls the world into being for us, along with everything else, including God. There is no satisfactory way out of this paradox. All the solutions we offer turn out to be versions of the same old problem. If there is God and a world out there, we can only know them, understand them, be in touch with them, through the agency of our own perceptions. This should promote neither despair at ever being able to get hold of anything outside our own heads, nor the kind of immobilising scepticism that believes nothing is knowable as it is in itself. What it does compel us to accept, however, is the creativity of human consciousness in the act of knowing anything, including God: that's where all the ladders start. If we accept that principle, it rules out naive realism, because that fails to take into account the contribution we ourselves unavoidably make to any encounter with reality.

As a matter of fact, when it comes to our interpretation of the New Testament, the same three approaches apply. Some people adopt an attitude of naive realism to the text, some an attitude of non-realism and, somewhere in the middle, is the group that adopts the position of critical realism. And this is where we encounter a major difficulty. Many believers are unaware of the range of different approaches to the interpretation of the Bible. They think that the only possible attitude for a Christian to adopt to the New Testament is that of uncritical acceptance of everything in it, so they are scandalised when they hear that there are a number of other ways of interpreting the text. At the other extreme are the people the nineteenth-century German theologian Friedrich Schleiermacher called 'the cultured despisers of religion', who dismiss any type of Christianity as a primitive mentality that is impossible for an educated person today. They despise religious thinkers who try to offer a contemporary understanding of faith and the scriptures on which it is based. 'The ones with real faith', they say of naive-realists, 'go on believing the impossible things we ourselves have rejected. They are magnificently deluded, but we admire them for their deluded sincerity. But as for the those who are trying to interpret faith in ways consistent with contemporary understanding, these are the ones we really despise.' Most New Testament scholars today support neither of these uncritical approaches to the New Testament. They adopt a position of critical realism. They believe that, although the New Testament puts us in touch with transcendent reality, it has been mediated through human communities that had an effect on its shape and content, so it requires interpretation.

Two great principles have been established by scholars in their interpretation of the New Testament today, though there are inevitable differences in their application. The first is that the early Church had an enormous part in shaping how the written tradition of Jesus has come down to us. In the New Testament there is a core of material that goes back to Jesus, mostly from his sayings and parables; but much of what we now have in the gospels is the result of the early Church's own wrestling with the meaning of Jesus, which is why we have to discriminate between what comes directly from Jesus and what is mediated through the Church. Let me use the fourth Gospel as an example.

The late Raymond Brown, a Catholic academic, was one

of the most moderate and scholarly interpreters of the Gospel of John in recent history. A man of enormous reverence, conservative in his attitude to Christian tradition, Brown was convinced that John's Gospel was produced by a Christian community that was in intense dispute with the local synagogue from which it was painfully beginning to separate itself. We know that Christianity began as a movement within Judaism, from which it ultimately separated. According to Brown, the fourth Gospel reflects the struggles of one group during those days, which accounts for its strong and fateful denunciations of 'the Jews', as though they were generic enemies of Jesus, rather than the community from which he and his earliest followers came. When we read John, we have to understand that we are listening to the result of the meditation of a group of Christians who have just separated, with much bitterness and mutual recrimination, from the local Jewish community. The long discourses in this Gospel are to be understood not as verbatim recordings of monologues by Jesus, but as complex theological interpretations of his meaning for the early Church. Understanding the Gospel in that way, we can put its claims in historical perspective.

The other general principle that is broadly accepted today is that much of the material in the New Testament is not history remembered, but prophecy historicised. This is a much more difficult principle to get hold of, because we would consider it dishonest to create stories in order to fulfil old prophecies. The biblical writers did not write abstract theology, they told stories heavy with symbolism and hidden meaning. They did not try to explain that Jesus was the fulfilment of the old Israel, they crafted narratives that put him right in the middle of Hebrew history. This is an ancient religious technique with a special name, 'midrash'. We still do it today, and C.S. Lewis's *Screwtape Letters* is a good example. If you were ignorant of Christian history and came across a copy of this book in five hundred years' time, you might get into a furious argument about its factual status, about whether the letters were actually written by one devil to another, when what you ought to get from them is their hidden message.

Once we grasp this literary distinction it gets us out of a number of dead-end controversies. For example, the birth narratives in Matthew and Luke are inconsistent with each other, so they can't both be historically true. But what if neither is making historical claims, but both are making theological claims about the significance of Jesus? Then they can both be right. For instance, it is likely that Matthew has in mind the struggle among Jewish Christians about whether to remain in the young Church or revert to the synagogue. Using the midrash technique we have talked about, Matthew sets Jesus at the centre of Jewish history as its fulfilment or culmination. Just as the people of Israel were the victims of a wicked king who massacred Jewish babies, so was Jesus the target of a similar purge by Herod; and just as the Israelites went down into Egypt, and were brought out of slavery by Moses, so Jesus flees into Egypt, and returns after Herod's death to fulfil his destiny. The point of the story is to place Jesus in the prophetic, Mosaic tradition of the Hebrew scriptures.

Scholars debate endlessly over these matters, but the point I am trying to establish here is that scriptural interpretation is more dynamic and improvisational than naive realism or literalism. By depriving people of insight into the different approaches to biblical interpretation, because we are afraid of upsetting them, we are driving others out of the Church who mistakenly believe that naive realism is the only deal on offer. This is one of the most significant issues confronting the Church today; and how we respond to it will determine the fate of Christianity in the complex and sophisticated culture of northern Europe in the twenty-first century.

The twentieth-century American composer Aaron Copland once said that we were in need of 'a usable past', and his compositions, such as 'Appalachian Spring' and 'Fanfare for the Common Man', capture the sweep and struggle of American history. We live our lives forwards but understand them backwards, so it helps us to negotiate our journey if we have maps from the past to guide us. They are the traditions of our forebears, their memories and reflections on how they made their own journey and understood its meaning. Education is the way we pass on the tradition. Societies which have achieved stability and duration do this by inculcating acceptance of a group narrative that both interprets and directs every aspect of the human journey.

But Copland's usable past comes in different forms. We have all encountered people who are proud exemplars of powerful traditions. There is the strong conservative male, perhaps a high-ranking officer in a uniformed profession such as the police or the army, who has completely internalised the tradition that bred him, and may have risked his life in its defence. People in these guardian roles are often equipped with a high practical intelligence, but they are rarely reflective or open to doubt; so they can be intolerant of reformers, whom they usually dismiss with colourful contempt. Further down the chain of authority from these brave personalities we find the more naive members of traditional communities. They are usually shallow beneficiaries of the prevailing system who do little to protect or extend it, apart from offering it their uncomprehending benediction.

One of the paradoxes of human development is illuminated here. The duration of a tradition is important to societies that prize stability and continuity, but its very immobility can threaten the existence of the tradition itself, because it inhibits its evolution and development. The strong protectors of a tradition can end up as fundamentalists whose resistance to change puts the tradition itself at risk. An example of this is provided by a row that erupted in the Anglican Communion in March 2023 over the issue of the blessing of gay relationships in church services. Though some provinces in the Anglican Communion now permit full gay weddings – such as the Episcopal churches in the United States of America and in Scotland – the Church of England has characteristically adopted a hesitant compromise that allows gay unions to be blessed, but not yet married according to the official rites of the Church. For many, this may look like a distinction without a difference, but it has provoked the anger of a number of Anglican provinces in Africa, which are now threatening schism over the compromise. Like all schismatics, they claim not that they are leaving the Anglican Communion, but that it has left them. As one them has claimed: 'The Church of England has now departed from the Anglican Faith and are now false teachers.'

We don't yet know how this will play out and whether some kind of compromise will be achieved, compromise being the aim of the current Archbishop of Canterbury in negotiating the issue; but it provides us with a classic example of how difficult moral evolution is for faith communities that claim to be in possession of a sacred text that makes the moral norms of a previous age fundamental to its self-understanding. Over the last fifty years in the worldwide Anglican Communion, we have seen this theme play itself out over the equality of women, where similar scriptural prohibitions were quoted in opposition to the move to give them parity with men. Finally, the necessary compromises were made and the change to the status of women in the Church went ahead, though it also prompted the departure of many from the Anglican Communion because they believed the change was unscriptural. In time, a similar result may be achieved in the case of gay relationships; but it may not, and a real schism may occur. It has happened before. It has been a pattern in all faith traditions from time immemorial, which is why the history of religion is a story of constant tumult and the raising of voices and the slamming of doors. It is the name of the game.

But history also shows that it is those who have the courage to deviate from the tradition who provide the energy for its development and continuance. The people who are persecuted for their heresy and lack of fidelity to the tradition may be the agents who preserve whatever is sound in the tradition and give it enduring life. A deeper version of the same paradox is that the founders who become the passionate focus of fundamentalist loyalty in a later era were almost always heretics in the original historical context, as was the case with Jesus. The prophets who ignite new faith systems were all persecuted as heretics for their original inspirations. Nietzsche recognised this pattern of struggle in human history. The values we learned to prize and take for granted almost all began as heresies that were once abominated.

> Do you think that every good thing has always had a good conscience? . . . The good conscience has as a preliminary stage the bad conscience – the latter is not its opposite: for everything good was once new, consequently unfamiliar, contrary to custom, *immoral*, and gnawed at the heart of its fortunate inventor like a work.[2]

All institutions need strong conservatives who work hard to preserve and transmit the traditions they have inherited from the past; but they also need the challenge of the heretics and radicals who help them adapt to necessary change and thereby guarantee them a continuing future. This creates a painful tension in the institution, but it is that very tension that is evidence of continuing life. To be alive is to struggle and change. The alternative is the graveyard.

8

WALKING AWAY FROM CHURCH

Many churches I know have walking groups that advertise their activities in the parish newsletter, accompanied by cheerful photographs of a dozen people in boots and gaiters waving at the camera from the summit of a hill. As I gaze at the copy and look at the photographs I shiver with apprehension, because they are my idea of a good walk wasted. Church walking groups are a blethery lot, but then so is the body they represent, which is why E.M. Forster sneered at 'poor little talkative Christianity'. Words are not the only coinage of religion, but they seem to be the dominant currency and some of us are weary of them. We are tired of hectoring voices telling us what to think about gay people. We are weary of prominent Christians complaining of being persecuted by rabid atheists who stalk the land, seeking whom they may devour. Come to think of it, we are just as bored with evangelical atheists as we are with their religious counterparts, which is why many of us, to quote Psalm 121, have started lifting 'our eyes unto the hills' as places of spiritual refreshment and personal renewal. We might even claim that walking has become the new church-going, the way we set apart time for a serious and reflective purpose that takes us out of ourselves into something greater than we are — the mysterious world of hills and mountains. This is a world that calls us from words into silence not because peching up a hill makes conversation difficult, but because silence is the best response to mystery. Walking hills and mountains brings us up against the mystery of 'Being', and the sense that there is something beyond us we can't quite step into. This is why the best nature writing takes us beyond the science of the countryside into a silence that sometimes feels like worship. Bruce Chatwin was a heroic walker who understood the spirituality of what he did. In a piece about the German film director Werner Herzog he wrote:

> He was the only person with whom I could have a one-to-one conversation on what I called the sacramental aspect of walking. He and I share a belief that walking is not simply therapeutic for one's self but is a poetic activity that can cure the world of its ills. In 1974, when he heard Lotte Eisner was dying, he set out walking through ice and snow, from Munich to Paris, confident that somehow he could walk away her sickness. By the time he reached her apartment she had recovered and went on to live another ten years.[1]

The sacramental aspect of walking! There it is again, the suggestion that walking is spiritually enriching, as good as going to Mass. Come to think of it, a good walk, a thoughtful walk, is not unlike the four-fold musical structure of the Mass, leading us deep into the human hunger for meaning and self-knowledge.

ON REFLECTION

We begin the service with the *introit,* the anthem that covers the entrance into the sanctuary: *I will go unto the altar of God.* Humans have been on the go from the beginning. Walking has been in our DNA since our forebears trudged out of Africa into history. Chatwin said the reason walking helps a fretful child sleep is because there is a deep memory in humanity of being strapped to our mothers' backs while we plodded across the steppes and tundra of our pilgrimage through time. Think of the great migrations, the most celebrated being the exodus of the Israelites from Egypt, followed by forty years of wandering in the wilderness before reaching their Promised Land. And think of the human impulse to challenge evil by *marching* against it. Spool in your head the silent film of the Jarrow marchers; or recall the determined walk of Ghandi to the sea to defy the Raj's Salt Tax; or remind yourself of the noisy tumult of the millions who marched against the folly of the Iraq War in 2003. Humans are walkers with a purpose, ever on the go, moving through time and space, searching for the Promised Land.

While it is true that our walking has been full of purpose, it has also been a search for consolation. The first thing we do when we enter the sanctuary in church is to sing the ancient prayer *Kyrie eleison* in which we pray for the soothing mercy of God. Walking is consoling. We go on to the hills to clear our heads, get them straight, get things into perspective and cease our fretting. There's even a Latin tag for it, *solvitur ambulando,* which means 'solved by walking'. And walking precipitates the bittersweet consolation of memory. As we walk we remember other walks: walks when we were young, clutching our mother's hand;

walks with lovers into the shelter of concealing woods; walks with our children before they walked away from us into their own lives; and walks with friends who have made the last journey into death. As I walk nowadays, these are the kind of memories that spool through my mind, fortifying me with the knowledge that, since I too will one day take my last walk, I should make time now to be glad I can still lift my head to these brooding hills.

The Bible is full of gladness when it describes nature, and it says that the hills themselves jump with joy. I live near some primary schools in Edinburgh, so I see a lot of children being led to their classes by parents, and I am always delighted to notice that, while the parents trudge with their heads down, the children *skip!* They do it out of sheer gladness at being alive, *joie de vivre*. This is the third mood walking impels in us – *rejoicing*. The most exultant music in the mass comes during the *Sanctus*, when the choir shouts out Holy! Holy! Holy! This is the feeling that used to overcome me when I made it to the top of Scald Law in the Pentlands, while I still had the legs for it, and saw the Forth spread out before me to the north and Stevenson's hills of home flowing away from me into the misty south: *holy holy holy!*

Poets like Wordsworth called this feeling *sublime*, but it's not a word I like. It means to lift up or exalt, and it suggests the declamatory pose of the traveller braying his appreciation of a wonder of nature. I once stood by the Grand Canyon listening to a group of tourists ejaculate their compliments into the wind, and I longed for them to fall silent. Nature should deepen our thinking not prompt us to strike poses before it. Deepen is the right word here.

ON REFLECTION

The Jesuit poet Gerard Manley Hopkins got it right when he meditated on how we had abused nature with our greed and ugliness but had not defeated it:

> And all is seared with trade; bleared, smeared with toil;
> And wears man's smudge and shares man's smell: the soil
> Is bare now, nor can foot feel, being shod.
>
> And for all this, nature is never spent;
> There lives the dearest freshness deep down things . . . [2]

That *dearest freshness deep down* should provoke love in us, the love of a child for her parents. Though our big brains and the obsessions they provoke tend to separate us from nature – a tendency that is exaggerated in urban cultures – we all come from the earth and to the earth we shall return. As far as we know, it is only on this tiny blue speck among the grey intergalactic spaces that life has burgeoned. If you look back at the glowing earth from Space it is obvious that our planet is alive. Nature is our mother, not our plaything – and children should cherish their mothers and be grateful to them for the gift of life.

And we should not shrink from the pain that suffuses the earth. Beneath the serenity of a sunlit afternoon on our favourite hill, nature is red in tooth and claw. One aspect of Christian worship is its refusal to hide from the suffering of the world. The fourth element in the music of the Mass meditates on the Lamb of God that takes away the sin of the world. Walking the Pentlands in the lambing season, my heart always rejoiced as the lambs skipped before me, but I made myself remember the meat in my freezer at home. I am a predator, like most animals on the planet: others die that I may live. So while nature gladdens us, it also saddens us. The writer who understood this best was J.A. Baker. One year, from autumn to spring, he followed a pair of peregrines across the fenlands of eastern England. Enthralled by their fierceness and beauty, he refused to sentimentalise them.

> I shall try to make plain the bloodiness of killing. Too often this has been slurred over by those who defend hawks. Flesh-eating man is in no way superior. It is so easy to love the dead. The word 'predator' is baggy with misuse. All birds eat living flesh at some time in their lives. Consider the cold-eyed thrush, that springy carnivore of lawns, worm stabber, basher to death of snails. We should not sentimentalise his song, and forget the killing that sustains it.[3]

Baker was so aware of the careless brutality of humans, compared to the swift fierceness of nature, that he began to hate his own species:

> No pain, no death, is more terrible to a wild creature than its fear of man . . . A poisoned crow, gaping and helplessly floundering in the grass, bright yellow foam bubbling from its throat, will dash itself up again and again on to the descending wall of air, if you try to catch it. A rabbit, inflated and foul with myxomatosis . . .

will feel the vibration of your footstep and will look for you with bulging, sightless eyes. We are the killers. We stink of death. We carry it with us. It sticks to us like frost. We cannot tear it away.[4]

Here, he is excoriating our proneness to excess, and the way we have destroyed the balance of life on our planet. Walking reflectively can lead to repentance, but we need to understand the meaning of the word and purge it of its pious associations. It means to change our mind and turn it round, the way racists might own their prejudices and banish them, or the way homophobes might admit their hatred of gays comes from fear of their own unacknowledged desires. Walking becomes a metaphor for spiritual change, for leaving something behind – and sometimes it hurts.

My own walking led me to a painful re-evaluation of religion. Humans are notoriously prone to disagreement on every subject under heaven, but there is something particularly toxic about religious disagreement, because it allows us to hold our point of view not as one opinion among many others but as the unalterable truth of God. As a matter of fact, history shows that the mind of God is constantly changing – or we are constantly changing our minds about the mind of God. God once allowed slavery, but that changed in the eighteenth century and we banned it. God once commanded the subordination of women to men, but that too started changing a few years ago, though not all religions have caught up with the change.

What I came to understand in walking Scotland's hills was that none of this had anything to do with God and everything to do with us. Religion is as human as politics and every bit as fallible and volatile. Let us value it as a story we have told ourselves to help us live well and more kindly, and stop using it as an excuse for hammering people who differ from us in the way they choose to live the brief life they have been given. And brief it is, too brief to waste bashing others. Take a walk instead.

9

EXILE

When I hear the word *exile*, I think of the English writers Alan Bennett and Graham Greene, for both of whom it is a persistent theme. Being prone to homesickness and melancholia, it is a theme I am interested in. I am moved by the thought of the person exiled from home, pining for the dear, lost remembered place. I have been unable to track it down, so my memory might be playing tricks on me, but one of the most poignant moments I can remember from my boyhood – too much of which was spent in the local picture house – was of a standard Hollywood adventure movie featuring Clark Gable as a criminal living abroad, somewhere in the East, who is unable to return to the USA because of charges hanging over his head. He possesses a scratchy old recording of rush hour on Broadway in Manhattan, which he plays to himself from time to time. What we hear is the revving of engines, the hooting of horns, the blowing of whistles, the grinding of gears, the mad cacophony of midtown madness in New York: what he hears is home, the place where his heart longs to be again.

Bennett, with greater skill and subtlety, captures the same note in his 1983 TV play *An Englishmen Abroad*.

EXILE

Based on a true incident, it concerns an encounter between Coral Browne, in Moscow to act in a play, and the traitor Guy Burgess, exiled there after his defection from Britain. They meet several times, and the conclusion of the play is that she arranges to have a Savile Row suit made for and sent out to him in Moscow. The point I am reaching for comes during one of their conversations in his flat in a brutalist-style high-rise housing development – filmed, incidentally, in a hideous Scottish tower-block – when he asks her what the cricket is like in England these days. And you feel his sudden stab of longing for home, the place R.S. Thomas described as 'the glimpsed good place permanent'.

Graham Greene is also a poet of exile, with a deeper, more tragic vision than Bennett's. He claimed for himself some lines from *Bishop Blougram's Apology*, by Robert Browning:

> Our interest's on the dangerous
>   edge of things.
> The honest thief, the tender
>   murderer,
>   The superstitious atheist . . .

Greene's most interesting characters all live on that dangerous edge; never quite belonging anywhere, they live in a state of permanent exile. Most of them are double-agents of one sort or another, traitors to the values that nurtured them. His novel, *The Human Factor*, is about a double-agent, Maurice Castle, who is forced to defect to Russia in the middle of the Cold War, leaving his wife and son behind in England. She is an African, very ill at ease in England, but prevented from joining her husband because there is a threat to make her son a ward of court if she tries to leave. At the end of the book, he exiled in Russia, she in England, they manage to speak on the phone:

> 'We needn't go on pretending any more. They'll always be listening.'
>
> There was a pause. She thought he had gone away or that the line had been cut. Then he said, 'I miss you terribly, Sarah.'
>
> 'Oh, so do I. So do I, but I can't leave Sam behind.'
> 'Of course you can't. I can understand that.'
> 'When he's a little older . . .' It sounded like the promise of a distant future when they would both be old. 'Be patient.'
>
> 'Yes – Boris says the same. I'll be patient.'
> She asked, 'Have you friends?'
> 'Oh yes, I'm not alone, don't worry, Sarah. There's an Englishman who used to be in the British Council. He's invited me to his dacha in the country when the spring comes. When the spring comes,' he repeated in a voice which she hardly recognised – it was the voice of an old man who couldn't count with certainty on any spring to come.
>
> She said, 'Maurice, Maurice, please go on hoping,' but in the long unbroken silence which followed she realised that the line to Moscow was dead.[1]

Burgess and Castle are traitors to their homeland, forced into separation from it. It is worth pausing here for a minute to savour that word traitor. For most of us it has a smell we don't like – betrayal, unfaithfulness, ingratitude. In Christianity we have a technical word for it: apostasy. Apostates no longer stand alongside us: they stand elsewhere, stand against us. And we reserve our bitterest hatred for those who have gone out from us to stand in a different place. But bear two things in mind: treason, apostasy, whatever you call it, takes courage, moral as well as physical courage. Traitors, like radical disciples of Jesus, are grasped by an idea that overrides every other loyalty and for which they are prepared to plunge themselves into the agony of separation.

> If any man come to me, and hate not his father, and mother, and wife, and children, and brethren, and sisters, yea, and his own life, he cannot be my disciple.
>
> – Luke, 14:26

Courage and intensity of that sort makes the timid shiver with anxiety at the cost of such discipleship. But there's something else here I want to notice: in human history, it is the disloyal, the apostates, on whom moral progress and evolution depend. If we were all permanently and invincibly loyal to the systems and institutions that enclose us, there would never be social change and moral evolution. As I have observed before, this was one of Nietzsche's most daring insights:

> History teaches that a race of people is best preserved where the greater number hold one common spirit in consequence of the similarity of their accustomed and

indisputable principles: in consequence, therefore, of their common faith. Thus strength is afforded by good and thorough customs, thus is learnt the subjection of the individual, and strenuousness of character becomes a birth gift and afterwards is fostered as a habit. The danger to these communities founded on individuals of strong and similar character is that gradually increasing stupidity through transmission, which follows all stability like its shadow. It is on the more unrestricted, more uncertain and morally weaker individuals that depends the intellectual progress of such communities, it is they who attempt all that is new and manifold. Numbers of these perish on account of their weakness, without having achieved any specially visible effect; but generally, particularly when they have descendants, they flare up and from time to time inflict a wound on the stable element of the community. Precisely in this sore and weakened place the community is inoculated with something new; but its general strength must be great enough to absorb and assimilate this new thing into its blood. Deviating natures are of the utmost importance wherever there is to be progress. Every wholesale progress must be preceded by a partial weakening. The strongest natures retain the type, the weaker ones help it to develop.[2]

Let me offer an obvious example to illustrate the truth of this insight. The emancipation of women would never have taken place if all men had remained loyal to the ancient institution of patriarchy. So, why has the liberation of women been glacially slow in religious institutions?

Because religions prize faithfulness and obedience so highly, and loathe apostasy so passionately, they have erected enormous transcendental obstacles to change. I'll come back to the moral importance of apostasy for social evolution later: meanwhile, let me return to the pain it causes the apostate.

This pain is born of the divided love of traitors or apostates for the institutions that nurtured them, but which they have now betrayed. Because of a higher or competing loyalty, they have been forced to leave the place they loved, but their departure does not destroy their affection for it. They continue to miss it, but they know there can be no going back. One of the most moving and eloquent expressions of this kind of homesickness for the abandoned place came from Cardinal Newman as he looked back on his exile from his beloved Oxford, the price he paid for converting to Roman Catholicism:

> Trinity had never been unkind to me. There used to be much snap-dragon growing on the walls opposite my freshman's rooms there, and I had for years taken it as the emblem of my own perpetual residence even unto death in my university. On the morning of the 23rd I left the Observatory. I have never seen Oxford since, excepting its spires, as they are seen from the railway.[3]

So far, I have been thinking about the cost of exile paid by the apostate; and I have hinted at the moral importance of such emigrations. Traitors are people who have made painful exits from institutions they loved and for which they suffer an enduring attachment.

Let me turn now to a more radical kind of exile, which I'll call ontological exile. There are always people who remain permanently outside all the enclosures of organised society, because they refuse to accept the compromises that ordinary institutional life demands of them. What is it about institutions that prompts this kind of radical rejection by some of the most interesting and creative people in human history? I want to begin my answer by referring to something the great German sociologist Max Weber said: he talked about 'the routinisation of charisma', and I want to think for a bit about that inelegant but helpful phrase. Whenever an idea is born, a moral, religious, artistic or political vision, it usually comes through the charisma or giftedness of an individual of genius. (Incidentally, they are often the same people that Nietzsche talked about in the passage I have already quoted: the degenerates, the heretics, the experimenters, the inventors of the new.) Unless the new thing is to die with the one who gave it birth, it has to be given a body that will carry it further into history. In Weber's language, a routine; in the language of this essay, an institution. It is here that we begin to observe the paradox inherent in this process: the vehicle, the routine, the institution that carries the new idea and gives it enduring life, also begins to stifle it. This is because institutions have their own laws, and their first law is the moral primacy of the institution itself.

The late, great New Testament scholar Raymond Brown gave a series of lectures before his death that illustrated the power of this law. He was talking about the birth and evolution of the Christian Church, in Weber's language, the routine that evolved to give enduring life to the charisma of Jesus. In an introductory lecture he explored the paradox of this process, the contradiction of any institution representing or claiming to embody the profoundly anti-institutional genius of Jesus. He gave a couple of amusing examples. No competently managed farm would employ a shepherd who routinely left ninety-nine sheep unprotected while he went off and hunted for the one that was lost. No Chief Executive Officer of any company would hire a manager who forgave embezzlers not seven times, but seventy times seven. Neither institution could survive an ethic as insane as that. Not even the Christian Church can operate on that kind of pure grace. The Christian Church works by the logic that governs all institutions, the logic of its own survival, the logic of general laws. The paradox is that it does this in the name of one who was not interested in his own survival, who was indifferent to institutional generalities, and saw only the tragic reality of unique individuals. Something that the Russian philosopher Nikolai Berdyaev said could be applied to Jesus's unswerving commitment to the individual: 'Creative morality is that attitude which states that it is impossible to judge any matter ethically unless it is taken as being a unique case.'

Every sinner is a unique case, but most of us don't see them like that: we care more for the good of the forest than the fate of the individual trees; we rate the health and survival of the institution higher than the welfare of individuals within it who have collided with the system. Jesus did not see things like that, which is why he was loved by the sinners who had been ejected by the system and loathed by the ejectors. So, isn't it strange to have him represented by a body that is governed not by the insanity of grace, but by the laws of institutional survival?

And there is another paradox that is just as important. It is true that the Church has never followed Jesus with this kind of absoluteness, but it has kept the memory of Jesus alive in history, much the way a healthy body can carry a defect it passes unwittingly on to others. If Jesus is the supreme example of the charismatic outsider who lived in a state of permanent exile from the ethic of institutional life, there have always been others like him, few in any generation, but enough to keep his uncomfortable example alive. I would like to think about one of them, already mentioned in a previous essay.

She was one of the most remarkable women of the twentieth century and she starved herself to death in an English hospital on 15 April 1943. She was being eaten up by tuberculosis, yet she refused to consume more than the daily ration of a prisoner in a concentration camp. Her name was Simone Weil. She was a disciple of the French philosopher Alain, who committed himself to rethinking everything, based on the reading, each year, of one philosopher and one poet. Alain claimed to belong to the eternal Left, the Left that never exercises power, because by nature power always abuses the individual. These words echo Lord Acton's famous claim that 'power tends to corrupt and absolute power corrupts absolutely'. This means that people of the eternal Left who refuse to exercise power remain exiled from all human institutions, because, whatever else they are, institutions are always systems of power. You could say that power was the main subject addressed by Simone Weil. I am deeply disturbed by what she wrote about power, but let me first look at her definition of the word.

Here is what she said: 'To define power or force – it is that X that turns anybody who is subjected to it into a thing.'[4] Power is that which turns us into things, makes us objects. It is significant that these words were written by a woman, because the experience of objectification, of being turned into a thing, has been one of the most constant elements in woman's relationship with a world that has always been controlled by male power. Describing the dehumanising experience of uninvited sex, for instance, Simone Weil said: 'To assume power over is to soil. To possess is to soil.' To be objectified in this way is to say to yourself, 'I am no longer myself, me, this person, this human-being. I have been turned into a thing for someone else's use.' Nothing is more violating to the self, nothing more killing to the spirit. Not only is your body being raped, your soul is being stolen, your identity is being destroyed. Rape may be at the extreme end of this experience of objectification, of being turned into a thing, but there are lots of other notches on the continuum down to being whistled at in the street. Germaine Greer pointed to the way that kind of sexual objectification switches in a woman's later life to a kind of invisibility, though it is the same principle at work: the woman is robbed of her personal identity and becomes a thing, whether visible or invisible.

Every man, certainly every straight man, will recognise that accusation. Even the spiritual power-system of the celibate priesthood has objectified women and bent them into the shape it preferred, queen of the kitchen, mistress of the shining floors, the mother who for ever remains a virgin. As Lord Acton put it, power always corrupts. That was the devastating conclusion that Simone Weil came to: anyone in a position of power abuses it. We might kid ourselves that, since we know how dangerous a drug it is, when we get power – in a personal relationship, in a family in any sort of community – we will be the exception and avoid corruption. According to Simone Weil, there are no exceptions. The authorities she cites in support of this chastening conclusion are the poet Homer and the prophet Jesus. She wrote a remarkable essay on the *Iliad*, in which she claims that the depth of Homer's tragic vision of the way power destroys us was only ever equalled by Jesus. Homer, full of pity, sang darkly of the way power takes men over and robs them of sanity and proportion. You only have to think about the Homeric violence of the wars that continue to rage in our time to feel the abiding truth of his lament over human folly. Simone Weil ends her essay on the *Iliad* with these words: ' . . . there is no refuge from fate, but we can learn not to admire force, not to hate the enemy, nor to scorn the unfortunate.'

That was also the message of Jesus: he said 'No' to power and might. Like Homer, he knew there was no refuge from these forces and their sway over humans, but he refused to be a part of the system that did the ruling. His refusal was about much more than turning the other cheek, or refusing to take up arms. He knew that the corruptions of power go deeply into the soul; he knew how the mighty bewitch and seduce the heart.

EXILE

It is worth noticing how, in the company of the famous and powerful, people bend themselves physically into a different shape. You only have to look at the photographs in the papers of people being introduced to members of the British royal family to see the obsequiousness that melts their features, and the awkward genuflections they offer that distort the shape of their bodies. To be in the presence of the powerful evaporates their inner strength and turns them into toadying nonentities; the aura of power melts their moral skeleton and turns them into things.

'But it shall not be so among you,' said Jesus, in his meditation on power in Mark, Chapter 10. He advised his friends not to admire power nor to be seduced by those who hold it. That was why Simone Weil, though she loved Jesus, never became a Christian. To her, the Church was just another power system, another way of pushing people around. To the end she belonged to Alain's eternal Left that refused ever to exercise power over others. She wrote:

> In my eyes Christianity is Catholic by right but not in fact. So many things are outside it, so many things I love and do not want to give up, so many things that God loves, otherwise they would not be in existence. All the immense stretches of past centuries, except the last twenty, are among them ... all the traditions banned as heretical; all those things resulting from the Renaissance, so often degraded but not quite without value.[5]

ON REFLECTION

Insights like that made Simone Weil, like Jesus, a permanent outsider, someone who refused to be recruited into any of the world's power systems, an eternal exile.

This is a challenging insight and one that is almost impossible for lesser mortals to practise, given the way power gets hold of us, seducing where it cannot bully, and bullying where it cannot seduce. Most of us succumb at some time in our lives to the protective lure of the institution. We may even rationalise what we are doing as the price we pay to get things done in a world of power, so we accept the pragmatic necessity of our own corruption. And there is truth in that tragic insight. It is the logic of the Grand Inquisitor in Dostoevsky's greatest novel *The Brothers Karamazov*.

During the Inquisition in Spain, where heretics are being burned at the stake for disobedience to ecclesiastical power, Jesus comes to Seville and walks through the city. People instinctively recognise him and seek his counsel, so the Grand Inquisitor has him arrested, and comes to visit him in his prison cell. He delivers a monologue in which he points out to Jesus that people do not want the terrifying freedom he has offered them. They want the security and protection of a power system, including all its necessary compromises. They will never be able to follow Jesus's way of freedom and compassion.

> . . . when the Inquisitor fell silent, he waited for some time for his prisoner to reply . . . He had seen how the captive listened to him all the while intently and calmly, looking him straight in the eye, and apparently not wishing to contradict anything. The old man would have

liked him to say something, even something bitter, terrible. But suddenly he approaches the old man in silence and gently kisses him on his bloodless, ninety-year-old lips. That is the whole answer. The old man shudders. Something stirs at the corners of his mouth; he walks to the door, opens it, and says to him: 'Go and do not come again . . . do not come at all . . . never, never!' And he lets him out into 'the dark squares of the city'.[6]

Yes, there is that to justify those who accept the necessary corruption of office and power. But there are always some who don't; flinty, demanding people, few at any time, who turn the searchlight of their purity on to the excesses of the powerful. They are artists, comedians, poets, prophets, who mercilessly expose the corruption of power and the way it abuses and objectifies humanity. Like the poet Homer, like the prophet Jesus, like the philosopher Simone Weil, they know there is no refuge from the world of power and its excesses, but they refuse to admire it or bow before it. They are society's eternal exiles, the ones who absolutely refuse to come in from the cold.

And to return to my Nietzschean paradox: it is these incorrigible heretics, these permanent outsiders, who bring change to the very institutions they are in exile from. From their place of exile they send the future into the past and inoculate the old with the new, so that what was once dismissed and despised, gradually becomes accepted and admired. Nietzsche called this the 'transvaluation' of values, their turnaround, their adaptive reversal. It sounds like the things Jesus said: the first will be last, the last first;

the greatest will be the least, the least the greatest; woe are you when men speak well of you; blessed are you when they hate and despise you. Upside down and downside up. No wonder the New Testament scholar John Dominic Crossan called the Jesus movement a kingdom of nobodies and undesirables. The way into it is the way out of it – not belonging, but exile.

Yet for those of us who do not have the courage to face such loneliness there remains some comfort. We may look into our hearts and realise with a pang, that we need to be somebody, need to be desirable, need some kind of power. Jesus doesn't say anything. He steps forward and kisses us . . .

10

SECULAR FAITH

In the mists that obscure the origins of Judaism, Christianity and Islam there lurks a mysterious character called Abraham, which is why these three great monotheistic faith systems call themselves Abrahamic religions. The Book of Genesis tells us that Abraham was the patriarch who begat Isaac, who begat Jacob, who begat the Twelve Tribes of Israel, who ended up as slaves in Egypt, whence Moses led them into history. However obscure Abraham was, and however uncertain the facts about him are, he bequeathed to the three religions that claim him as their forebear an ancient practice that is baffling to the modern mind: he listened to a Voice in his head to which he accorded absolute authority. It tells us a lot about religion and why many are wary of it today. The text in question is found in Genesis, Chapter 22:

> And it came to pass after these things, that God did tempt Abraham, and said unto him, Abraham: and he said, Behold, here I am. And he said, Take now thy son, thine only son Isaac, whom thou lovest, and get thee into the land of Moriah; and offer him there for a burnt offering upon one of the mountains which I will tell thee of.

Today, we would medicate someone who heard a voice issuing an order like that, but in Abraham's time it was an essential requirement for the founder of a religion. The origins of religion are as hazy as the origins of Abraham himself, but one educated guess is that when early humans started talking to themselves in their own heads, the way we all do, they assumed that it was someone else who was on the line. This gave rise to a binary or bifurcated view of reality, resulting in what historians of culture call the bicameral mind: the theory that one part of the brain speaks and another part listens and acts. The voice in the head that is an inescapable aspect of the experience of consciousness was projected outwards and given an independent objective reality; and dreaming was accorded a similar authority. Here is Nietzsche on the subject:

> Misunderstanding of Dreams. — In the ages of a rude and primitive civilisation man believed that in dreams he became acquainted with a second actual world; herein lies the origin of all metaphysics. Without dreams there could have been found no reason for a division of the world. The distinction, too, between soul and body is connected with the most ancient comprehension of dreams, also the supposition of an imaginary soul-body, therefore the origin of all belief in spirits, and probably also the belief in gods. 'The dead continues to live, for he appears to the living in a dream': thus men reasoned of old for thousands and thousands of years.[1]

Much of the time this does not matter. If the Voice commands us to perform certain ritual acts and refrain from certain foods, that is something we easily adapt to. The dietary or ritual side of religion is not a problem. If the Voice had confined itself to dietary restrictions and ritual practices, we would not give it a second thought. It is the fact that the Voice told Abraham to kill his son that gives us pause.

Having been a religious practitioner most of my life, I have acquired the survival skill of theological interpretation of stories like this; but it took a secular novelist to open my eyes to the horror that others see lurking behind religion's abstractions. The standard theological interpretation of the story of Abraham's obedience to the Voice that commanded him to sacrifice his son is to see it as a splendid example of faith. I was taught to admire the absoluteness of Abraham's obedience, because he was prepared even to kill his son for the sake of the Voice. Obedience to God should override every other loyalty, I was taught. And by that standard, Abraham was a paragon of faith. What rocklike obedience! But what about Isaac? Where does he figure in the story? Did the Voice of God consult him before using him as a device for testing his father's faith?

It was not a theologian who made me ask these questions; it was a novelist who was appalled by the stories religious people so unthinkingly pass on to each other. In her novel, *After These Things,* Jenny Diski imaginatively explores the human side of these divine interactions. In particular, she gets inside the head of Isaac, the unconsidered object of his father's trial of faith. As Abraham hung over him, about to cut his throat, Isaac must have realised that he lived in a dangerous and unpredictable universe, in which a son might be sacrificed to the demands of a voice in his father's head that was more powerful than human love. Or to put it another way, don't trust a believer, even if he is your father. That is the devastating insight that makes the secular mind anxious about the unpredictable power religion has to plunge people into madness. How can you negotiate the intricacies of living alongside people who are programmed by an invisible, inaudible voice? We know the Voice is still at work, calling its servants to kill their children and ours in obedience to an allegiance that is more powerful than any human bond. We see it there three thousand years ago in the pages of the Old Testament; and we see it here in the pages of our newspapers today. The Voice still speaks and Abraham's children still obey its command. The bombs go off, killing innocent people out for the evening, unaware they are the target of the Voice, oblivious to its anger. *The Terror of Isaac*, the Bible's name for God in the Book of Genesis, is still in business, messing with people's heads.

There have been interesting developments since Abraham's time. The Voice of God has been institutionalised by religious authority and no longer speaks directly to private individuals. The authorities who take over a religion once it has established itself are suspicious of people who claim to hear the Voice of God speaking to them directly, even though they are the kind of people who get religions going in the first place. A bishop of the Church of England said to one who heard such voices, 'Sir, the pretending to extraordinary revelations and gifts of the Holy Ghost is a horrid thing, a very horrid thing.'[2] That is why the leaders who took over the Abrahamic faiths de-privatised the Voice and replaced it with an authorised translation of its original utterances. The advantage of this was that it gave the spiritual leaders more control over their followers than would have been possible had they been allowed direct access to the Voice of God. The official theory was that, though there had been a time, an original dispensation when God communicated directly with inspired individuals, that time was over. The Direct Line had been disconnected, but this was not a problem. During the period when God had been online, issuing directions concerning all that humanity needed to order its life, everything had been recorded, so all we have to do now is open the file containing the original transaction, read it and obey.

This is progress of a sort. We can now read for ourselves what the Voice said, and that's a gain. We no longer have to rely on sacred figures who might suddenly tell us that the Voice spoke to them last night and ordered the sacrifice of our children. We've got everything in writing now, and the great thing about words on a page is that you can argue endlessly about what they mean. Words in books are subject to different interpretations. That's why, in addition to the Holy Books themselves, over the centuries other volumes have accrued round them, offering us a variety of approaches to the original revelation. As is the way with these things, these secondary texts achieved a hallowed reputation and became subject, in their turn, to interpretation. This constantly ramifying process gave rise to a vast scholarly industry called theology.

By this point it should be obvious that, attractive as it might at first appear to have a Holy Book, it turns out to be far from straightforward, because its interpreters are prone to disagree with each other. History teaches that each separate religious tradition has been a hotbed of rival interpreters who have anathematised and sometimes killed each other over rival interpretations of the sacred text. That is bad enough, and it makes religion look like a dangerously unpredictable business to get involved with. But there is worse to come. If it is hard enough deciding which school of interpretation within a particular religious tradition to follow, how are we to choose between the different religions themselves? They may be coy about expressing their exclusivity today, but in the past, they bluntly warned us that only their route could successfully bypass Hell and safely carry us to Heaven. *Extra ecclesiam nulla salus* – there is no salvation outside the Church, said an influential Christian bishop in the year 258 CE.

The arrogant exclusivity of the different religions is confusing enough for the honest searcher after truth, but there is something else we ought to look at before moving on. First let me summarise the story so far. We are invited to believe that a divine voice once spoke authoritatively to certain men of spiritual genius – always men – who obeyed its dictates, no matter how cruel they were. Apart from the gruesome story of Abraham and Isaac, which religious commentators now rationalise as the moment where humanity turned against human sacrifice, there is the equally grim narrative of Israel's settlement in the Promised Land after a genocidal campaign against its original inhabitants, all at the prompting of God. This ancient narrative is still a major element in the lethal cocktail of Middle East politics. We are also told that although the voice no longer speaks directly to humans, it has left us an authoritative written account of the original conversation. But we soon discover it is subject to different interpretations. Worse, there are rival versions of the message itself, each claiming primacy over the others.

That is the confusing religious situation that faces humanity, so it is not surprising that many have given up on the whole business. How are they expected to pick their way through this minefield of competing claims? Its history of strife and rivalry makes issues of choice in religion problematic enough, but there is another major difficulty that really clinches the matter for many of us today. Each record of the original revelation is old, and it shows. Sticking only to the Abrahamic religions: one goes back 3,000 years, one goes back 2,000 years, one goes back 1,400 years. Are we seriously meant to understand that we have to run our lives today according to systems devised back then in such totally different circumstances?

Let us look at the difficulty I keep returning to: the role and place of women in religion and society. You don't have to be a historian to know that back in the days when these revelations were recorded, societies were patriarchal systems, run by men for men. Women, for reasons that may have made sense at the time, were a protected and subservient species. That has changed in most secularised societies. Social evolution and effective methods of contraception have given women more control over their lives, a fact that is reflected in their political and economic status in modern societies. The equality of the sexes is a fundamental value throughout secular European society. What is interesting here is that faith communities with theological objections to gender equality are allowed to maintain their discriminatory laws within their own boundaries.

Though modern societies have banned discrimination against women on account of their gender, they permit religious communities to practise this ancient form of discrimination within their own communities. In Britain today a woman can sue her local Hospital Trust if its employment policies discriminate against her, but she cannot sue the Roman Catholic church for refusing even to consider the possibility that she might become a priest. It is worth noting here that discrimination against women in Christianity has been identified as one of the important precipitating factors in the freefall in church attendance in Britain since the 1960s.[3] And the revulsion felt against religion by people who are committed to the equality of women has been fortified by the debate in the churches over the moral status of homosexuals. The homophobia of orthodox Christianity has served to widen the gulf between the emancipatory ethic of European society today and the authoritarian approach of most of the Christian churches.

What this adds up to is that today most people in Europe recognise that religions are definitionally stuck in the past. The main difficulty confronting faiths that base themselves on an authoritative revelation from God delivered thousands of years ago is that it effectively cuts them off from the current of human development that is the most pronounced characteristic of our reflective species. Their problem is a consequence of what seemed, at the time, to be a brilliant idea: the establishment of an official record of God's instructions to humanity in a holy book. This wouldn't matter so much if the instructions had been benignly vague, such as the command to love our neighbours and other helpful generalities. Unfortunately, the holy books go in for more detailed prescriptions than that. In effect, they freezeframe the social arrangements of thousands of years ago, informing us that God has commanded them to be followed forever. That is why traditional religions have a hard time dealing with the movements for human emancipation that have been such an important part of the European moral tradition since the Enlightenment. If the Voice of God has infallibly declared that women are inferior and subordinate to men, and that homosexual relations are an unnatural abomination, they are going to have a hard time living in societies in which gender and sexual equality are fundamental values. Generous-minded observers try to sympathise with the difficulty religious people have in dealing with these changes. They know that social evolution is a fitful and untidy process. They realise that history is a machine in perpetual motion, and we can't stop the engine and start the whole thing over again every couple of generations. They know we have to learn to live with inconsistent and incompatible values in open societies. A good example of this is the magnanimous way secular society has adapted itself to religious groups for whom history ended a long time ago. And this is a useful place to turn to the slippery word I brought in to that sentence, *secular*.

It comes from the Latin *saecularis*, pertaining to a *saeculum* or age. An example of its original use was the *ludi saeculares* in ancient Rome, the secular games, so called because they took place once a *saeculum* or every hundred years. Like everything else about humanity, language is dynamic and never stays put, and the history of this word is a case in point. The distinction that started to emerge was the one between time and eternity, between the world, where everything was in constant flux, with age succeeding age; and Heaven, where there was no successiveness, only an endless present, a single changeless moment where no shadow was cast by turning.[4] By the Middle Ages the term secular, in its various forms, was being used to refer to the world and its transient order, in contradistinction to the Church, which was thought of as an outpost of Eternity on Earth, though even here the distinction was not absolute. For example, by the twelfth century it was usual to talk about two types of ordained clergy, secular and regular. Regular clergy were monks or members of religious orders, living in religious houses, while secular clergy lived in the world and looked after the laity as their pastors.

The development that finally established the existence of a profound gulf of sensibility in humanity's interpretation of reality was the coinage of the word secularism in 1851 by G.J. Holyoake. He used the term to denote a system which sought to interpret and order human life on principles derived solely from this world, without reference to God or any other invisible source of authority. Holyoake wanted human ethics to be based on what was measurably good for humanity, not on the basis of obedience to an invisible inaudible voice. He would have told Abraham that he was mad to listen to the voice in his head rather than to the obvious claim upon his affections of his son. Holyoake may have coined the term *secular*, but the dynamic that lay behind the movement it described had been building since the Enlightenment, that extraordinary revolt of the eighteenth century against the intolerance and divisiveness of religion. One of the most characteristic voices of the Enlightenment was Voltaire's. He was an advocate not only of the value, but also of the necessity of tolerance in human affairs. And his reasoning was interesting. In his *Philosophical Dictionary* he warned us that we are all formed of weakness and error, so we should reciprocally pardon each other's folly. Shall a reed laid low in the mud by the wind say to a fellow reed fallen in the opposite direction: 'Crawl as I crawl, wretch, or I shall petition that you be torn up by the roots and burned'?[5] It was obvious to Voltaire and other thinkers of the Enlightenment that revealed religions were incapable of this magnanimity. They were *intrinsically* intolerant; intolerance was essential to their self-understanding. Believing, as they did, that they were in possession of the final and absolute truth communicated directly to them by God, how could they possibly tolerate those who spurned it? That is why they were always authoritarian when they held untrammelled sway in a society.

Secular consciousness drew two important conclusions from the disruptive effects on human society of the intrinsic intolerance of religion. The first was that the authority of religious leaders had to be confined to their own faith communities: Church and state had to be separated. This process of separation happened in different ways and at different speeds in Europe, and was never perfectly achieved anywhere, though it probably came closest in France where everything in the public realm was constitutionally established as fully secular. It was a more untidy and gradual process in England, where Church of

England bishops sit in the House of Lords and take part in the parliamentary process without any democratic mandate from the electorate.

But it was the second element in the secular strategy that had the greater impact: the outlawing of religious discrimination and intolerance. This enabled the emergence of religious pluralism in European societies, with an inevitably eroding and relativising effect upon the authority and influence of any single religious denomination. Voltaire said that if you have two religions in your land, they will cut each other's throats, but if you have thirty religions, they will dwell in peace.[6]

I think Voltaire was being too magnanimous. Religions are adept at taking advantage of the tolerance that secular governments extend to them, but they rarely return the compliment. If you believe that your point of view is not just another human opinion, but comes directly from an all-knowing and all-powerful God, then you will believe that you have not only the right, but the duty to impose it on everyone, everywhere, whether or not they share your beliefs.

A much more dangerous example of the same dynamic is what Malise Ruthven called the transcendentalising of human conflict.[7] Politics is a messy and inexact business, which relies on pragmatic compromises by its practitioners if there is to be any forward momentum in human affairs. By definition, convinced religious believers do not believe in compromise. If you possess divine truth, how can you compromise it by negotiating with the children of darkness? This is why fundamentalists always transcendentalise worldly disputes. There are many examples of this phenomenon today, the turmoil in the Middle East being the most conspicuous. But there are other examples, one of the most worrying being the takeover of the once sober and steady US Republican Party by fundamentalist Christian groups who refuse to practise the arts of political compromise, because of the Voice they hear in their heads. A similar pattern of interreligious conflict is emerging in the Indian sub-continent, where even Hinduism, a traditionally tolerant and eclectic religion, is assuming violent and fundamentalist forms. Though the resurgence of religious intolerance in the world today confronts humanity with fateful challenges, we have been here before. The philosopher George Santayana warned us that those who cannot remember the past are condemned to repeat it.[8] The last time religious conflict threatened to overwhelm human wellbeing, Europe responded by returning religion's evil genie of intolerance to its bottle, though it did not, perhaps, bang the cork in tightly enough.

That is what we have to do again. We have to reassert the secular spirit that established tolerance as a fundamental value of civilised society. We have to tell religions that they are welcome in our midst, as long as they confine their disputes to their own sphere. They can fume and boil inside their own bottles, but we will not let them overflow and flood the human community with their poisonous certainties. More positively, we can use the religions themselves as allies in the cause of promoting a truly tolerant society. Sophisticated religions always develop within the parameters of their own self-understanding, so that radical change is experienced not as disjunctive, but as evolutionary, as the realisation of values that are innate within them. It could even be argued that the emergence of tolerance as a fundamental human value was the fruit of the biblical hatred of the abuse of human power. Protest and dissidence can be seen as children of the Hebrew prophetic tradition, which knew that false gods were always more dangerous than no gods. It is worth remembering that, as well as being vehicles for ancient prejudices, religions have also been carriers of important human values, such as justice and mercy. It could even be argued that the best elements of secular society are a humanised distillation of the wisdom of the biblical traditions. That is why there is room for guarded optimism. As well as being a part of the problem that faces humanity today, religion could also be part of the solution.

11

GRIEF

They say that when you get to the final phase of old age your life comes back to you during the night in dreams, sometimes in regret, sometimes in gratitude. That is certainly what is happening to me, and it is aided by my fondness for volumes of diaries and collections of letters, all describing what is over and done with and gone into the past. All we can do now is revisit the dear, dead past either by remembering it or by leafing through old photograph albums showing how things were.

But what are we mourning when we mourn the passing of time? The poet Gerard Manley Hopkins said we were mourning ourselves, mourning our transience:

> Márgarét, are you gríeving
> Over Goldengrove unleaving?
> Leaves, like the things of man, you
> With your fresh thoughts care for, can you?
> Ah as the heart grows older
> It will come to such sights colder
> By and by, nor spare a sigh
> Though worlds of wanwood leafmeal lie;
> And yet you will weep and know why.

ON REFLECTION

> Now no matter, child, the name:
> Sorrow's springs are the same.
> Nor mouth had, no nor mind, expressed
> What heart heard of, ghost guessed:
> It is the blight man was born for,
> It is Margaret you mourn for.[1]

Typing out that Hopkins' poem now has brought back memories. On the flyleaf of the book I copied it from I find this writing:

> Richard Holloway, Accra, June 1956

I bought it from the University Bookshop in Achimota, Accra, in what was then still the Gold Coast, a colony of the British Empire, till it became independent the following year, as Ghana. The edition of the collection is itself significant. As well as being a great poet, Hopkins was a Jesuit priest, though never a happy one, and none of his poetry was published in his lifetime. As the introduction to this collection describes it: 'Gerard Manley Hopkins died in 1889 and rose again as a living poet in 1918.' It was his friend, the Poet Laureate Robert Bridges, who brought about his resurrection by gathering his friend's poems together, complete with Hopkins' own stresses and accents on them, intended to assist the reader to recite them in the rhythms of natural speech. For example, in Hopkins' version of this text, the first lines of the poem are printed like this; and that is how Hopkins wanted us to read it.

GRIEF

Márgarét, are you grieving
Over Goldengrove unleaving?

What Hopkins called 'the blight man was born for' is our grief at the passing of time and the way it takes everything from us, including, at the end, our own life. It is significant that the title of the poem is: 'Spring and Fall: To a Young Child'.

Margaret — or Márgarét — is mourning the falling of the leaves in autumn, but Hopkins tells her it is her own finitude, her passing-ness, that she is really mourning.

I suspect that it is this mourning for lost time that lies behind the conservative temperament and its urge to preserve what it can of the past. The torrents of time wash so many things away from us that we long for some of them to endure, especially the good things we ourselves discovered or created. This is one of the reasons we are sent to school. The classical function of education is the orderly transmission of the best of human culture from one generation to the next. In his 2006 play, *The History Boys*, Alan Bennett calls this function of education 'passing the parcel', and he puts these words into the mouth of Hector, the history teacher:

> Pass the parcel. That's sometimes all you can do. Take it, feel it, and pass it on. Not for me, not for you, but for someone, somewhere, one day. Pass it on, boys. That's the game I want you to learn. Pass it on.

You get a strong sense of the power and effectiveness of this approach if you visit the ancient private schools, where the sense of passing on a tradition is palpable, and powdery-skinned teachers get misty-eyed as they look back on the generations they have taught, all rolling up to school reunions in their Bentleys and Jaguars. In certain moods I not only feel the attractiveness of this conservative attitude to life, this passing-on of a cherished tradition, I sympathise with the moral imperative that lies behind it. Why not try to protect some of the things we have loved from what Shakespeare called 'cormorant devouring Time'? Time gets us all in the end, but why appease the monster, why not resist him, why not disdain the dizzy multitude who dance to his tune?

The paradox is that we ourselves are the agents of the changes we find it so hard to adapt to and so difficult to keep up with. We are constantly unsettled by our own cleverness and its ability to tear up the cultural environment and refashion it every generation, which is why we develop our own counter-intelligence network of social and religious institutions to be a bulwark against change. A conservative attitude to the institutions we have built to protect us from the ravages of time seems to be wise as well as prudent. It is no accident that the conservative temperament is frequently associated with the religious attitude to life, the sense that some important traditions have been delivered to us from beyond ourselves to be kept safe so that they might keep us safe. Jesus was not immune to this sense that the old ways were precious and should not be lightly abandoned:

No man having drunk old wine straightway
desireth new: for he saith, the old is better.

— Luke: 5–39

However, there are a couple of important difficulties with this reverence towards the institutions which the past has bequeathed to us. The first is that someone, somewhere, has to pay the tax for the upkeep of these bulwarks against change, and it is rarely the people who derive benefit from them. This is the most enduring and effective element of Marx's critique of human power relations. He observed that powerful institutions always defend themselves, with force as well as theory. He noticed that behind the reverent appeal to changeless tradition there often lies something uglier, which is the ruthless determination to hold on to power for its own sake. As I have already noticed on a previous page, a much more surprising insight comes from Nietzsche, who was no friend of egalitarianism. In 'Human, All Too Human', he writes:

> History teaches that a race of people is best preserved where the greater number hold one common spirit in consequence of the similarity of their accustomed and indisputable principles: in consequence, therefore, of their common faith. Thus strength is afforded by good and thorough customs, thus is learnt the subjection of the individual, and strenuousness of character becomes a birth gift and afterwards is fostered as a habit.[2]

That's an excellent summary of the conservative educational imperative. But then Nietzsche goes on to offer one of his most important insights. He continues:

> The danger to these communities founded on individuals of strong and similar character is that gradually

increasing stupidity through transmission, which follows all stability like its shadow. It is on the more unrestricted, more uncertain and morally weaker individuals that depends the intellectual progress of such communities, it is they who attempt all that is new and manifold. Numbers of these perish on account of their weakness, without having achieved any specially visible effect; but generally, particularly when they have descendants, they flare up and from time to time inflict a wound on the stable element of the community. Precisely in this sore and weakened place the community is inoculated with something new; but its general strength must be great enough to absorb and assimilate this new thing into its blood. Deviating natures are of the utmost importance wherever there is to be progress. Every wholesale progress must be preceded by a partial weakening. The strongest natures retain the type, the weaker ones help it to develop.³

It is important to understand the use of the terms degenerate and morally weak in Nietzsche. There is always an undercurrent of irony in what he says, so we ought to understand the terms from the point of view of the strong guardians of the tradition in question. In Nietzschean language, the strongest natures will have accepted the traditional system most completely and will operate within it unselfconsciously. From their point of view, any questioning of it is a sign of degeneracy. We have all encountered exemplars of powerful traditions, of both the strong and stupid types.

Nietzsche's insight is that it is those who challenge the

system, because of their proneness to doubt and reflection, who provide the means for its continuing development. One of the elements that contributes to social, political and moral evolution is the emergence of the difficult customer within the community, the transgressor who refuses to conform, the radical who starts to question the assumptions by which the powerful govern, the reformer who calls for changes in the way things are run.

We could develop a whole theory of society and the way it educates its young from that quotation from Nietzsche. A fundamental part of their education would be their initiation into the tradition of the community to which they belong, what Bennett called 'passing the parcel'. This is an essentially conservative process, which imparts the community tradition to the next generation and hands on to it the knowledge that has been accumulated by its best minds. The second part of the process, as expressed by Nietzsche, has to be the deconstruction of the tradition that has been previously internalised. You cannot move a tradition on if you have not mastered it, which is why the great innovators and revolutionaries have always absorbed the tradition that they later played such an important part in transforming. A complete education will involve both of these very different processes, one essentially conservative, the other essentially radical. It is the radical imperative I wish to concentrate on in this essay.

But first, here's a summary of where I have got to so far. Humans are a problem to themselves, because something in them craves changelessness and stability, the paradox being that they themselves are the agents of the change that causes them so much pain. That is why they establish systems and traditions to protect themselves against the flood waters of their own restlessness. But there are always injustices, sometimes implicit, sometimes explicit, in these fortifying systems, which gradually corrupt them and which, if ignored, threaten their own survival. The crowning paradox is that it is the heretics, the doubters and transgressors, whose relentless questioning and refusal to conform bring the future to these traditions and enable them to adapt and continue. Let me offer the normative example I keep returning to: the status of women.

Until fairly recently, the dominant institutions in our society, the great carriers of tradition, were male dominated. Their dominance was not considered to be incidental; it was held to be an intrinsic good, part of the self-understanding of the institutions in question. Male dominance was sanctioned by ancient tradition and divine revelation. But there came a point in the evolution of the status of women in our society when this male intransigence began to look not strong but stupid, to use Nietzsche's word. The question 'Why?' that was ceaselessly put to male dominance by the women's movement began to make the constant reply – 'Because God said so, and we agree with Him.' – look increasingly silly. In time, even men realised what idiots they were, and changes were made, changes that caused a radical social revolution in my lifetime everywhere – everywhere, with the exception of certain conservative religious institutions. One of the advantages of still having these conservative forms of religion around is so that we can point to them as living exhibits in the cultural museum of history. If your eighteen-year-old daughter, who refuses to be patronised by any male of the species, wants to know 'What it was like in the olden days, Mummy?', you don't have to invest in time travel to show her, because there are plenty of churches and mosques around that will do the job just as well.

But I need to offer a balancing observation here. When I talk about the radical questioning of human institutions that prompts them to evolve and adapt to the future, I am not necessarily claiming that this process always secures moral progress or human happiness. As a matter of fact, I believe that the emancipation of women was not only an irresistible social development, but also a considerable moral improvement on what went before. It has helped us to humanise and banish much of the cruelty that was endemic in many of our social structures. But social change always has its losses as well as its gains. This is why social conservatives mourn the loss of the traditional family, which has been the most conspicuous casualty of female emancipation, though the reasons for its evolution are complex.

The other balancing observation must be that the traditional family had a bleak and frequently brutal downside. The point to be grasped here is that, given our dynamic, restless nature as a species, social change is constant; so the issue is not whether to accept or reject it, but how best to manage it. By refusing to engage with change, by refusing to question the effectiveness or justice of received traditions, we not only endanger their survival, we may seriously corrupt them. There comes a point in the defence of the received system when it may become not just stupid to go on doing things the old way, but seriously damaging to the human community. If skilful living is more an art than a science, then we should be more intent on imparting to our children the kind of emotional confidence that will enable them to adapt to time and change. This is arguably less stupid than arming them with fixed and solid certainties that may break under pressure and therefore not help them navigate through the tides of history. To return to one of my favourite metaphors for adapting creatively to change, we need the ability to improvise that is the genius of the jazz musician. It is a suggestive model for human living that calls us to a certain lightness of being, an ability to adapt, to move, to change elegantly rather than awkwardly.

I suspect that in our culture we have inherited from Christianity some deep-rooted attitudes that make this improvisational approach difficult. For the classical Christian mind, nature and its imperious drives were problematic. Influenced by opinions that were around at the time it was forming its own traditions, early Christianity bought into the theory that the created order was fallen and intrinsically corrupt. There were always subtleties in the position, but they got lost, and Christians were left with some very damaging convictions. The most momentous of them was about sex, which was defined as a lamentable but necessary evil. Lamentable, because it gave pleasure and pleasure was always addictive; necessary, because without it the human species would die out. This did not stop some of the early fathers from pushing a scheme of universal celibacy in order to bring this wicked world to an end. It didn't catch on, and we were left with the idea that sexual pleasure was an evil that might be grudgingly licensed for occasional use in order to maintain the species, but was never to be enjoyed for its own sake. I think it is the presence of this neurosis deep in the collective unconscious of Christianity that has made it difficult for our culture to develop any idea of sexual love as an art, a human skill that calls for emotional intelligence.

Foucault compares our awkwardness here with classical Greek finesse. According to Foucault, for classical Greek thought, sexuality was potentially excessive by nature, so the moral question was how to control it, how to regulate its economy in an appropriate way. The regulated sexual economy was not achieved by a universal legislation that permitted or forbade certain acts, but rather by the achievement of an art of living that involved the individual in a battle to achieve dominion of the self over the self. This kind of self-overcoming was freely chosen for the sake of the self, just like any other discipline. The sexual act was not considered as a licit or illicit practice that had to be validated by external authority; it was viewed as an activity that could be more or less pernicious in its consequences, and should therefore be controlled and ordered. It was an act that demanded reflection and prudence, so it was not so much a question of right and wrong as one of more or less.[4] The underlying sense that the sex drive is not just something that needs to be managed with skill and sensitivity, but is itself problematic, still haunts our attempts to deal wisely with the subject.

Nevertheless, it is easy to understand why this profoundly pessimistic attitude to human sexuality developed. It is possible to romanticise the non-human creation, but there is a sense in which it is held in a kind of balance by the automaticity of its impulses. Animals kill to eat and to defend their territory; and they have sex to maintain their species. Unless we believe in some sort of divinely manipulated design in nature, we have to conclude that life itself has evolved or contrived these systems for the balanced maintenance of the species on the planet – with the exception of the human animal. There is something about the human animal that disposes it to inflated behaviour. Consciousness has endowed us with an element of transcendence over the purely instinctive side of our nature. This is why the Hebrew scriptures say we were made in the image of God: we have a level of freedom and understanding that allows us to override the automaticity of instinctive life. Richard Dawkins puts it like this:

> Stand tall, Bipedal Ape. The shark may outswim you, the cheetah outrun you, the swift outfly you, the capuchin outclimb you, the elephant outpower you, the redwood outlast you. But you have the biggest gift of all: the gift of understanding the ruthlessly cruel process that gave us existence; the gift of revulsion against its implications; the gift of foresight – something utterly foreign to the blundering short-term ways of natural selection – and the gift of internalizing the very cosmos.[5]

That is well said, but there is a dark side to the Bipedal Ape. Clever criminals are more dangerous than stupid ones. It is our cleverness, our ability to observe and understand, that makes us such dangerously unpredictable animals. We can use the gift of consciousness and understanding to direct our instinctive nature in a way that amplifies our humanity and the good of human flourishing. But we can also use it to gratify our own selfish greed and lust. This is particularly true in the area of human sexuality. History is full of examples of how powerful men used their power to achieve sexual gratification, usually at the expense of the weak. This is one reason why contemporary thinking about sexual ethics lays such stress on the principle of consent. There is much to be said for retaining some of the ancient religious pessimism about human nature and its proneness to excess, even if we want to sever it from its mythological base, though it is no surprise that religions developed myths of the Fall to account for humanity's mysterious capacity for destroying its own happiness by excess.

The other area of human pleasure that we have turned into a massive problem for ourselves is our use of euphoric substances – the trick here being to call the ones we don't ourselves use 'drugs'. Most human cultures use drugs for pleasure and escape, but we've got ourselves into a mess about the best way to manage this aspect of our humanity. We can take it absolutely for granted that, given our capacity for getting things wrong, many of us will use these substances unwisely some of the time; and some of us will use them unwisely all of the time. Driving through life is dangerous and many of us become casualties, but it does help if we've been given some training in managing the vehicle. Unfortunately, we smuggle into the discussion about drugs unadmitted assumptions about the moral status of the substances themselves. It's the same dualism we noticed with sex: some things are good, some things are evil; some substances are good, some substances are evil; some we will permit, some we will prohibit. Again, it comes down to 'Yes' or 'No', rather than 'More' or 'Less'; prohibition, rather than skilful living.

There is a utilitarian argument against the war on drugs that goes like this: 'It just doesn't work and it costs too much money and too many lives.' I am more interested in exploring the philosophical or metaphysical assumptions that undergird the present approach, here and in the USA. They are largely based on the kind of frightened puritanism that would rather ban things, because they are dangerous, than help us to manage them wisely and safely. The sad thing about all this is that any questioning of current strategies for dealing with sex and drugs is howled down by sections of the press and the political community. That shouldn't surprise us. Our fears and anxieties always erect vast fortresses of hypocrisy. The trick is not to try to blow them up, but to force their gates open by the insistence of our questioning. The most potent word in any language is the tiny interrogative: 'Why?' The freedom to question is not only a fundamental right, it is a moral imperative. It is a moral imperative, because without constant challenge our institutions and the powerful people who run them become corrupt. The freedom to question is probably the most distinctive and purifying characteristic of our species, but it can be dangerous. It got Socrates killed, but there are worse things to die for.

12

CREATING HELL

What are called 'doom paintings' are a dramatic feature in a number of medieval churches in England. One of the most famous is found in Saint Thomas's Church in Salisbury, dedicated to Thomas à Becket, the murdered Archbishop of Canterbury. Saint Thomas's is a beautiful, light and airy building, but high above the soaring chancel arch there is a terrifying doom painting on which demons with long forked tails are depicted, thrusting tormented souls into hell.

Though its fires are no longer stoked in mainstream Christian pulpits, the threat of Hell used to be one of the most effective weapons in the Church's evangelical armoury. I once heard the famous American preacher Billy Graham use it at a rally in Murrayfield Stadium in Edinburgh. As a psychological device it works by first developing a mood of self-contempt and dread in the listeners, as they are reminded of their sins and the punishment that awaits them after death, to be followed immediately by the offer of forgiveness and salvation – as long as they repent. At that point in his sermon, Billy Graham exhorted his listeners to: 'Just get up out of your seats and come forward', in order to lay hold of the salvation on offer. And hundreds did. But beneath the good looks and Southern charm of the famous preacher, the threat was still there, however veiled or implicit: 'or go to Hell', like the one painted on that chancel arch in Salisbury, depicting eager demons forking frightened souls into raging furnaces *that never went out*, the really terrifying feature of Hell being that if you were sent there, you would be there for ever and your torment would be without end! The Irish writer James Joyce remembered his Jesuit preachers laying the fear of Hell on thick, and without any of Billy Graham's charm:

> The torment of fire is the greatest torment to which the tyrant has ever subjected his fellow creatures. Place your finger for a moment in the flame of a candle and you will feel the pain of fire. But our earthly fire was created by God for the benefit of man, to maintain in him the spark of life and to help in the useful arts, whereas the fire of hell is of another quality and was created by God to torture and punish the unrepentant sinner. Our earthly fire also consumes more or less rapidly according as the object which it attacks is more or less combustible, so that human ingenuity has even succeeded in inventing chemical preparations to check or frustrate its action. But the sulphurous brimstone which burns in hell is a substance which is specially designed to burn for ever and for ever with unspeakable fury. Moreover, our earthly fire destroys at the same time as it burns, so that the more intense it is the shorter is its duration; but the fire of hell has this property, that it preserves that which it burns, and, though it rages with incredible intensity, it rages for ever.

Our earthly fire again, no matter how fierce or widespread it may be, is always of a limited extent; but the lake of fire in hell is boundless, shoreless and bottomless. And this terrible fire will not afflict the bodies of the damned only from without, but each lost soul will be a hell unto itself, the boundless fire raging in its very vitals. O, how terrible is the lot of those wretched beings! The blood seethes and boils in the veins, the brains are boiling in the skull, the heart in the breast glowing and bursting, the bowels a red-hot mass of burning pulp, the tender eyes flaming like molten balls.[1]

You can imagine the effect of a sermon like that on a congregation of adolescent boys. It was meant to act as a deterrent against masturbation, then called 'self-abuse'. A nineteenth-century Oxford don is said to have warned his congregation of young men: 'Why risk your eternal soul for the sake of a pleasure, which, I am reliably informed, lasts less than ninety seconds?' Even if you believed masturbation was a sin, there was a gross disproportion between the brevity of the offence and the eternity of the punishment. But in the Christian tradition there was more to Hell than a preventive against sin; it also doubled as a reward for the virtuous, an angle brought out by Nietzsche in one of his withering asides on Christianity. Describing the life of those in Heaven, he writes:

For what is it that constitutes the bliss of this Paradise? We might even guess, but it is better to have it expressly described for us by an authority not to be underestimated in such matters, Thomas Aquinas, the great teacher and saint: 'The blessed in the kingdom of heaven,' he says, meek as a lamb, 'will see the punishments of the damned, in order that their bliss be that much greater.'[2]

Hell provides both punishment and pleasure: it is torment for the damned who endure it, but bliss for the redeemed in Heaven who have the pleasure of observing their agony.

How can we explain the emergence and development of this, the grimmest of the great Christian myths? How did an idea of such cruelty develop in the way it did? The Protestant theologian Paul Tillich gave much thought to this question, and concluded that Hell was the mythical expression of our lived experience of what he called the '*structural power*' of evil. There is a type of mind that refuses to or is incapable of confronting the intractability of this kind of evil. It sees only 'individual acts of evil, dependent on the free decisions of the conscious personality'. And it believes 'in the possibility of inducing the great majority of individuals to follow the demands of an integrated personal and social life by education, persuasion, and adequate institutions'.[3] This liberal belief in progress and human perfectibility was destroyed for Tillich and other Christian Realists by the wars, revolutions and purges of the twentieth century – the most violent century in human history – assisted by humanity's emerging ability to explore the seething depths of its own psyche. Freud, Jung and Adler, the great analysts of humanity's psychic sickness, recorded their encounters with destructive forces within the human soul that determined the fate, not only of individuals, but of whole nations. Through their explorations of the unconscious forces within us, it was as if they were being offered a trailer or preview of the horrors that would soon erupt onto the conscious surface of history.

The tumults of the twentieth century forced Tillich to identify and confront two potent sources of evil in human history, which he labelled 'the Demonic'. One was the sleeping power hidden deep within our own psyche called the unconscious; the other was the herd instinct, the collective dimension of humanity that could possess and override the conscience of the virtuous individual. Together, these forces can create structures of evil that are well beyond the influence of the normal powers of personal good will. They promote individual and social tragedy of the sort witnessed throughout the twentieth century and which we continue to observe helplessly today.

As I type these words in the year 2023, as well as the civil war that has been raging in Syria for thirteen years, there has been a re-eruption of war in Israel–Palestine, and President Putin continues his aggression against Ukraine, using the same blitzkrieg tactics he used to flatten the historic cities of Syria. Our liberal impotence in the face of this kind of organised evil; our recognition that the institutions we create have a collective dynamic that can override the ethics of the individual; and our experience of the brutal reality of the group-mind, all remind us that there are systems of evil that are impervious to human decency and rationality. It is difficult to find a way of explaining these great forces without reverting to the theological. To use Tillich's term, they seem to be demonic, supra-human.

The weather systems that make life in the vast landmass

of the United States so dangerous and unpredictable provide us with a useful analogy. The hurricanes and twisters that wreak such damage on human settlements might lead an uneducated mind to supernatural explanations, and the story of Noah and the Flood in the Book of Genesis gives us an example. The Bible says the Flood was sent by God to 'destroy all flesh', because of the wickedness of the human race.

> And God saw that the wickedness of man was great in the earth, and that every imagination of the thoughts of his heart was only evil continually. And it repented the Lord that he had made man on the earth, and it grieved him at heart. And the Lord said, I will destroy man whom I have created from the face of the earth; both man, and beast, and the creeping things, and the fowls of the air; for it repenteth me that I have made them.
>
> – Genesis, 6:5–7

Thus, an outraged God unleashes the Flood on the earth:

> And every living substance was destroyed which was upon the face of the ground, both man, and cattle, and the creeping things, and the fowl of the heaven; and they were destroyed from the earth . . .
>
> – Genesis, 7:23

There was a flood as described there, but without the agency of an angry god to trigger it. There are accounts of a great flood in Babylonian and Sumerian chronicles, dating from around 19–1700 BCE, so it was clearly a devastating natural event to which a supernatural cause was attributed. Today, we don't need supernatural explanations, because science knows about the collision of weather systems that generate these spectacular forces, and can even predict them.

I am writing this not long after the earthquakes in Syria and Turkey in February 2023 flattened cities and killed tens of thousands of their citizens. We lament the death and destruction we are watching on our screens every evening, but we no longer attribute them to an angry god. We know about the shifting tectonic plates underneath the Earth's surface that can rise and cause such destruction. We may continue to pray for succour according to our traditions, but we also know that the sensible response is to construct quake-proof buildings in future.

We also know that human violence and war have been greater killers of humans in the modern era than natural disasters. The greatest killers have all been in the name of theories designed to rescue us from our miseries, which, instead, only magnified them. The philosopher Roger Scruton did not adopt Tillich's demonic label for this phenomenon, but he attributed to it the same frightening potency. He named it 'unscrupulous optimism', the belief that:

> . . . the difficulties and disorders of humankind can be overcome by some large-scale adjustment: it suffices to devise a new arrangement, a new system, and people will be released from their temporary prison into a realm of success.[4]

The main characteristic of these unscrupulous optimists in the modern era has been their ruthlessness. If it is the myth of Hell we are thinking about, then we saw it actualised in the twentieth century in a series of evils that could have been scripted by the author of *Genesis*, none worse or more archetypal than Hitler's Holocaust, the demonic destruction of six million Jews in the death camps of Europe. It was as if the Hell of the Christian theological imagination had realised itself in history and established itself as a crematory for Jews.

> . . . how terrible is the lot of those wretched beings! The blood seethes and boils in the veins, the brains are boiling in the skull, the heart in the breast glowing and bursting, the bowels a red-hot mass of burning pulp, the tender eyes flaming like molten balls.[5]

We no longer need to look at medieval doom paintings to get the picture. We've seen it all on television.

13

IN MEMORIAM

The poet Philip Larkin said the impulse to preserve lies at the bottom of all art. It is true that artists possess this capacity for recovering the past to an unusual degree, but the passion for making the past present again is a universal human characteristic. We are all artists in this sense. We do it all the time even if we'd never dream of describing it as art. Think of the conversations we hear on the bus as friends recount their day to each other. Even the endless football talk that dominates Scotland's air waves is a basic art form, as men bring back again the glory or shame of that afternoon's fixtures. While agreeing that one of the roots of art is this instinct to preserve the past, I sympathise even more strongly with its instinct to mourn lost time and protest its passing. Time steals everything from us, including our own lives and loves, so what I want to do here is offer a meditation on time, or indulge in a bout of handkerchief waving, in Alan Bennett's phrase, and I want to start at the movies.

One of the great arts of the cinema is the flashback, and it's a case of art imitating life: it is something we all do. We call back to mind, remember those we've loved and lost as the years sank into the past. I can still remember the flashback from a movie I saw in 1945 when I was eleven years old. It was called *The Fighting Sullivans*, the true story of a large Irish American family of sons, five of whom were killed in the Second World War. I was captivated by the series of flashbacks during the credits, showing the lives of the brothers before the war, and I was stabbed by a sense of time's passing. Michael Cimino used the same technique in the sequence at the end of his film, *The Deerhunter*, where the surviving friends go off to a bar and start singing 'God Bless America' as the screen flashes scenes of pre-Vietnam innocence. Films have made this kind of remembrance visual, but poetry was doing it long before movies were invented.

The best reason for being grateful to artists is that they name the terminal nature of our incurable disease, mortality. We are the only animals on the planet who know they are dying. Here's Dylan Thomas in 'Fern Hill':

> Nothing I cared in the lamb white days, that time
>   would take me
> Up to the swallow thronged loft by the shadow of
>   my hand,
> In the moon that is always rising,
> Nor that riding to sleep
> I should hear him fly with the high fields
> And wake to the farm forever fled from the childless
>   land.
> Oh, as I was young and easy in the mercy of his
>   means,
> Time held me green and dying
> Though I sang in my chains like the sea.[1]

IN MEMORIAM

If artists are trying to get us to pay attention, to look at life and love it and those it gave us before they are taken from us, then the writers I like to think of as artist–philosophers have a different role and prompt a different kind of mourning. They want us to reflect on the oddness of the human condition: we are beings who are aware of our own radical contingency and know we are dying. Of course, when their time comes, the other animals on the planet may not want to die either and fight against it. The poet Hal Summers captured the moment perfectly in a poem called 'My Old Cat':

> My old cat is dead,
> Who would butt me with his head.
> He had the sleekest fur.
> He had the blackest purr.
> Always gentle with us
> Was this black puss,
> But when I found him today
> Stiff and cold where he lay
> His look was a lion's,
> Full of rage and defiance:
> Oh, he would not pretend
> That what came was a friend
> But met it in pure hate.
> Well died, my old cat.[2]

The other animals may fight to hold on to their lives the way we all do, when they are threatened; but what they don't seem to do is live under the constant knowledge that time holds them 'green and dying'; that they are, in the language of existentialist philosophy, 'beings towards death'. Here is Blaise Pascal:

> When I consider the short duration of my life, swallowed up in the eternity before and after, the little space which I fill, and even can see, engulfed in the infinite immensity of space of which I am ignorant, and which knows me not, I am frightened, and am astonished being here rather than there, why now rather than then.[3]

That was a feeling Philip Larkin knew well. Margaret Drabble said of him that he reconciled us to our ills by the scrupulous way in which he noticed them. Yes, but Larkin himself was never reconciled to them. Here's a bit of his late, great poem, 'Aubade':

> I work all day, and get half-drunk at night.
> Waking at four to soundless dark, I stare.
> In time the curtain-edges will grow light.
> Till then I see what's really always there:
> Unresting death, a whole day nearer now . . .
> The sure extinction that we travel to
> And shall be lost in always . . .[4]

Naming your dread, the way Larkin does here, helps others name theirs and admit that they know what it is to lie awake contemplating 'unresting death, a whole day nearer now'. But there have always been some with no fear of death though they also knew it led to extinction. In the introduction to her novel about the Emperor Hadrian, the French novelist Marguerite Yourcenar expressed this ancient stoic attitude to death in these words:

IN MEMORIAM

> The melancholy of the antique world seems to me more profound than that of the moderns, all of whom more or less imply that beyond the dark void lies immortality. But for the ancients that 'black hole' is infinity itself; their dreams loom and vanish against a background of immutable ebony. No crying out, no convulsions – nothing but the fixity of a pensive gaze. Just when the gods had ceased to be and the Christ had not yet come, there was a unique moment in history, between Cicero and Marcus Aurelius, when man stood alone. Nowhere else do I find that particular grandeur.[5]

One theory of the origin of religion sees it as a refusal by humans to accept their finitude and the annihilation that follows death. So, whether in hope or in desperation, they craft works of art intended to defy death itself. One of the great poems of the defiance of death is Chapter 15 of Paul's First Letter to the Corinthians:

> Behold, I shew you a mystery; we shall not all sleep, but we shall all be changed, in a moment, in the twinkling of an eye, at the last trump: for the trumpet shall sound, and the dead shall be raised incorruptible, and we shall be changed. For this corruptible must put on incorruption, and this mortal must put on immortality. So when this corruptible shall have put on incorruption, and this mortal shall have put on immortality, then shall be brought to pass the saying that is written, Death is swallowed up in victory.

It is impossible not to be impressed by Paul's magnificent bombast, but I prefer John Donne:

> Death be not proud, though some have called thee
> Mighty and dreadful, for, thou art not soe,
> For, those, whom thou think'st, thou dost overthrow,
> Die not, poore death, nor yet canst thou kill mee.
> From rest and sleepe, which but thy pictures bee,
> Much pleasure, then from thee, much more must flow,
> And soonest our best men with thee doe goe,
> Rest of their bones, and soules deliverie.
> Thou art slave to Fate, Chance, kings, and desperate men,
> And dost with poison, warre, and sicknesse dwell,
> And poppie, or charmes can make us sleepe as well,
> And better than thy stroake; why swell'st thou then?
> One short sleepe past, wee wake eternally,
> And death shall be no more; death, thou shalt die.[6]

You have to admire the chutzpah behind Donne's defiance. For many that is all it is: an act of artistic resistance; but for others it is a confident assertion of faith; and even the faithless can learn from the gesture. Not believing it themselves, they can choose to live as if it were true because of the meaning it can give to their lives. This is the attitude we find in Miguel de Unamuno's great book about death, *The Tragic Sense of Life*:

> A time will come when this Universe and Nature itself will be extinguished. And just as of the grandest kingdoms and empires of mankind and the marvellous things achieved therein, very famous in their own time, no vestige or memory remains today, so, in like manner,

of the entire world and of the vicissitudes and calamities of all created things there will remain not a single trace, but a naked silence and a most profound stillness will fill the immensity of space. And so before ever it has been uttered or understood, this admirable and fearful secret of universal existence will be obliterated and lost.

Then he quotes Senancour:

Man is perishing; that may be; but let us perish resisting; and if it is nothingness that awaits us, let us so act that it will be an unjust fate.[7]

In other words, live as if there were a transcendent purpose to life, so that, even if the Italian philosopher Leopardi was right when he said that the weird experiment of being was empty of meaning from the beginning and was destined to be succeeded by a naked silence and a profound stillness, then we at least will have spoken words of purpose and love into the void, and we will have chosen to perish resisting. But isn't it strange that a universe that came from nowhere for no reason, gave birth to us, creatures with a hunger for meaning and a longing for purpose? And won't that make our purposeful transience greater than a universe that is destined to be obliterated and lost?

That's what keeps some of us active in communities of faith, though we no longer adhere to their creeds. We are practising but non-believing. Note that I describe us as *non*-believing, not *un*-believing. Convinced unbelievers are certain there is no ultimate meaning to existence. Life is an interesting accident they can enjoy, if they're luckily circumstanced, before it returns them to the void whence they came. And Convinced believers are just as certain of the opposite view: they *know* there is an ultimate meaning to life, and they are in on what it is. Certainty is the mark of both of these communities, whether it is the certain NO or the equally certain YES.

We non-believers lack that certainty. We are not sure if there is an ultimate meaning and purpose to the universe, but we choose to live as if there were. Our non-believing-belief may, indeed, be only an act of defiance against the meaningless universe that spawned and will destroy us. And yes, we may indeed be perishing, but we choose to perish resisting, and to live so that it will be an unjust fate!

14

MESSIAEN: QUATTUOR POUR LA FIN DU TEMPS

In Ridley Scott's 1982 sci-fi movie *Blade Runner*, a retired police officer called Rick Deckard, played by Harrison Ford, is hired to chase down and 'retire' biologically engineered humanoids called Replicants, who serve as soldiers and slaves in off-world colonies. To prevent them developing emotions and the longing for independence that might ensue, the Replicants have been engineered to have four-year lifespans, but it is feared that several of them have escaped to Earth to find ways to lengthen their lives.

The Replicants are built by the Tyrell Corporation, whose logo declares their product to be 'More Human than Human'. During an investigative visit to the Tyrell HQ, Deckard meets Rachael, played by Sean Young, an experimental Replicant who believes she is human, because her consciousness has been enhanced with memories from the life of Tyrell's niece. Rachael is devastated when Deckard tells her that she is not what she thinks she is. Her memories are not real, they are implants. She is not Human. She is a Replicant. Sean Young perfectly captures the anguish of Rachael's doubts about her own identity.

ON REFLECTION

At its best science-fiction has the power of myth, to explore the dilemmas of the human condition, so when I was invited to provide a short meditation as a prelude to a performance of Messiaen's 'Quartet for the End of Time', I was not surprised when a scene near the end of *Blade Runner* sprang into my mind, but before I come to it, let me offer a preliminary reflection.

It is well known that Messiaen's great work was composed and first performed in a prisoner-of-war camp in which he was interned during the Second World War. I am not surprised that it was prompted by the extremity of this experience, and I find the reason in some mysterious words in T.S. Eliot's fourth Quartet, 'Little Gidding', where he writes . . .

> There are other places
> Which also are the world's end, some at the sea jaws,
> Or over a dark lake, in a desert or a city –
> But this is the nearest, in place and time . . .'[1]

What I take him to mean is that there are certain extreme experiences in life that bring us to a threshold of revelation or disclosure – moments when we get the meaning that has been eluding us. Eliot's 'places which are the world's end' are what philosophers call 'liminal' moments, from the Latin for threshold. They are points of collision or grinding where our hunger for meaning comes up against the dissonance of evil. A prisoner-of-war camp is one of these places at the world's end or at the end of time. What Stalag VIII-A prompted in Messiaen was a defiant enunciation of his faith, expressed in his famous quartet.

MESSIAEN: QUATTUOR POUR LA FIN DU TEMPS

Finding yourself at the end of everything can do that for people of faith. It provokes a great shout of 'Nevertheless!' Nevertheless, in spite of the evil you do, there is a mercy greater than your cruelty; and when the universe is rolled up like a carpet and we come to the end of time, this truth will be shown to have triumphed over your lie.

The end of time is a difficult idea to get our heads around, probably because it is more a theological than a scientific concept. Strictly speaking, it is impossible to think about time on its own; instead, we have to think of the universe as a space–time continuum that seems to keep stretching in both dimensions. In God's eternity, it is claimed, that does not happen. There – if we can even call it 'there', because there is no there there – there is no successiveness, no duration, everything is all-at-once and all-together. To get remotely near that idea, try to think of the last time you were unaware of time because you were so out of yourself in the moment that you did not notice it. Maybe that is the experience Messiaen and his colleagues had in the camp as music took them out of the misery and boredom of successiveness into an eternal now. That was the defiance of faith captured in Messiaen's quartet, and for people of faith it continues to hold.

But what if you also find yourself at an end – wherever or whatever it is – and do not possess Messiaen's faith and the capacity to proclaim his 'Nevertheless!'. What word can you then honestly say at the sea jaws? I think there is such a word, but to find and utter it I must take us back to the parable of the *Blade Runner* and Rachael's dilemma. Rachael discovered that she was not who she thought she was. That is what happened to religion in the nineteenth century. Under the influence of millennia of religious teaching, humanity – let's call her Rachael – got used to thinking of herself as a special creation made in the image of God and destined to spend eternity with Him in Heaven. Darwin destroyed that uniqueness the way Deckard destroyed Rachael's; but in doing so Darwin bequeathed to us a tragic new uniqueness: which is the knowledge of our own finitude and the certainty of our own death. It is only death that will rescue us from the tyranny of time.

But what a waste that will be! Animals we may be, not immortal souls, Replicants not angels, but think of what will be lost when we go! As well as the horrors we have visited on the earth and the prison camps we have built, think also of the music we have composed, the cathedrals we have erected and the poets who have broken our hearts by the beauty of their words. Yet all this will come to an end and be as if it had never existed.

And here is my scene from *Blade Runner*. Roy the magnificent Replicant, played by Rutger Hauer, instead of killing Deckard, yanks him up beside him onto the ledge of the high building on which they have been fighting. It is raining relentlessly. Roy feels his powers waning. His four years are just about over. Wistfully, he looks back on his brief life, which has fled swifter than a weaver's shuttle. Then he says,

> I've seen things you people wouldn't believe. Attack ships on fire off the shoulder of Orion. I've watched C-beams glitter in the dark near the Tannhäuser Gate. All those moments will be lost in time, like tears in rain. Time to die.

MESSIAEN: QUATTUOR POUR LA FIN DU TEMPS

So, let me leave you with a thought. Whether you are, with Messiaen, able to utter the 'Nevertheless!' of faith as you come to your end, or whether, like Roy the Replicant, you believe that all your moments will be lost in time, like tears in rain, there will have been music, and who knows whether it will ever come to an end.

15

THE MUTILATED WORLD

In 1897 Paul Gauguin the painter received the news in distant Tahiti that his daughter Aline, back in Holland, had died of pneumonia. In response he produced a massive painting that was an anguished cry at the mystery of existence. He wrote three questions on the canvas:

> D'où Venons Nous? Que Sommes Nous? Où Allons Nous?
> Where do we come from? What are we? Where are we going?

Unlike the other animals with whom we share the planet, humans seem to be alone in being an object of interest to themselves, and the meaning of their own existence seems to many of them to be an unanswerable riddle. Of course, many confident answers have been given to Gauguin's questions – some, but not all of them, by religion. The trouble is that most of them were given when we knew hardly anything about the universe in which we find ourselves. Imagine that a man of sixty-five, with a long and complex history, wakes up in a strange hospital, remembering only the previous twenty-four hours, and has to make sense of his own existence on the basis of his memories of that one day. That's one way to think of the human predicament: until fairly recently we had to answer the questions life brings on the basis of remembering only a tiny fraction of the actual history of the universe – the 6,000 years of the creationists, who are literal believers in the chronology of the Old Testament, as opposed to the billions claimed by modern science.

Given the state of human ignorance about the origin of the universe until science unlocked its memory, religion's answers to Gauguin's questions were the best ones going. The atheist philosopher Daniel Dennett agrees that religion served – and may still serve – a useful purpose in trying to explain things; the trouble is – apart from the fact that the main religions were all established during that period of ignorance – he thinks religions always overdo it. He claims that this is because of the presence in all animals – and particularly in the human animal – of what he calls, borrowing the phrase from psychologist Justin Barrett – a hyperactive agent detection device, or HADD. He says this type of overshooting or overdetecting is not confined to humans:

> When your dog leaps up and growls when some snow falls off the eaves with a thud that rouses him from his nap, he is manifesting a 'false positive' orienting process triggered by his HADD.[1]

He claims that the false alarms generated by our overactive disposition to look for agents is the irritant around which religion grew. We can imagine what it must have been like for our distant forebears when their self-consciousness flickered into life, as they stared out from beneath their heavy brows at the mystery of existence. It may also account for the streak of cruelty that runs through primitive religion and is still found, however carefully articulated, in its more advanced forms. Whether or not it is the beginning of wisdom, as the Book of Proverbs claims, the fear of God was certainly the beginning of religion.

Today we have an acrimonious stand-off between two great responses to Gauguin's questions. Religion asserts that we came from the mind and creative intention of a supernatural agent we call God, which demands our obedience to its laws; and that our final destination is eternal life with It in the bliss of heaven, if we obey Its laws, or eternal life in the torment of Hell, if we disobey them.

Scientific atheism answers Gauguin's questions with equal confidence. It tells us that we came originally from an originating event called the Big Bang; that we are an accidental aggregate of molecules, blessed and afflicted with consciousness; that we are destined to return to that molecular state at death; but, since we ourselves will no longer be there to notice it, it won't bother us.

I have difficulties with both these responses to the mystery of existence, but dogmatic religion bothers me more than dogmatic atheism, not so much because of the omniscient confidence with which it answers what I deem to be unanswerable questions, but because of the way its answers lock us into the norms of ancient societies. I don't mind people telling me confidently that they know God exists. I mind strongly when they tell me God hates queers and wants women kept in their place, three paces behind their male controllers, with their heads suitably covered.

And dogmatic science bothers me, not so much because of the confident way it has unlocked the physical mysteries of the universe, but because of how it dismisses any attempt by religion to offer a different interpretation of itself in response to the emergence of new knowledge and ways of understanding the world: which is what Dennett does. He says:

> I define religions as social systems whose participants avow belief in a supernatural agent or agents whose approval is to be sought. This is, of course, a circuitous way of articulating the idea that a religion without God or gods is like a vertebrate without a backbone.[2]

I resist being limited by dogmatic religionists or dogmatic scientists in the way they respond to religion. I have no desire to convert anyone to my point of view, but I do insist on being religious in neither of the ways defined in this Punch and Judy show. For me, religion, like art, is a human creation, a work of the human imagination; and, again like art, it can be held to carry its own meaning within itself without any necessary reference to any other dimension that may or may not exist. I like what Howard Jacobson said in his novel *Kalooki Nights*:

> ... art is not the rendering of what is outside art ... art sees but remakes what it sees, in that way causing something to appear that wasn't there before.[3]

While I can no longer give confident answers to Gauguin's questions, I remain in awe of the mystery of existence, and I want to remain open to its surprises. That is why I don't respond sympathetically to the rival determinisms of big religion and big science. But something I read in Richard Mabey's book *Nature Cure* does feel right to me. He quotes at length from Joseph Meeker's book, *The Comedy of Survival*:

> (Evolution itself) proceeds as an unscrupulous, opportunistic comedy, the object of which appears to be the proliferation and preservation of as many life forms as possible. Successful participants in it are those who live and reproduce even when times are hard and dangerous, not those who are best able to destroy enemies or competitors. Its ground rules for participants, including people, are those that also govern literary comedy; organisms adapt themselves to their circumstances in every possible way, must studiously avoid all-or-nothing choices, must seek alternatives to death, must accept and revel in maximum diversity, must accommodate themselves to the accidental limitations of birth and environment, yet compete successfully when necessary . . . Comedy is a strategy for living that contains ecological wisdom, and it may be one of our best guides as we try to retain a place for ourselves among other animals that live according to the comic way.[4]

In his discussion of this passage, Mabey points out that:

> The ultimate expression of the comic way is play, an almost universal phenomenon among more complex animals (and which includes what humans call art), and

one which, in its exuberant purposelessness, seems close to the heart of the whole business of life.

All players are equal, or can be made so. Boundaries are well observed by crossing them. Novelty is more fun than repetition. Rules are negotiable from moment to moment. Risk in pursuit of play is worth it. The best play is beautiful and elegant. The purpose of playing is to play, nothing else.[5]

Play, art, exuberant purposelessness — these can promote love of life and of those others with whom we share the planet — and they can even make a kind of sense out of sorrow and loss. There's a passage at the end of Alan Hollinghurst's novel, *The Line of Beauty* that sums this up for me. Nick, who is waiting for the result of an HIV test, is walking away from the Feddens's grand house in Notting Hill. This is how the book ends.

> It came over him that the result would be positive. The words that were said every day to others would be said to him, in that quiet consulting room whose desk and carpet and square modern armchair would share indissolubly in the moment . . . He dawdled on rather breathless, seeing visions in the middle of the day. He tried to rationalize the fear, but its pull was too strong and original. It was inside himself, but the world around him, the parked cars, the cruising taxi, the church spire among the trees, had also been changed. They had been revealed. It was like a drug sensation, but without the awareness of play. The motorcyclist who lived over the

road clumped out in his leathers and attended to his bike. Nick gazed at him and then looked away in a regret that held and glazed him and kept him apart. There was nothing this man could to do help him. None of his friends could save him. The time came, and they learned the news in the room they were in, at a certain moment in their planned and continuing day. They woke the next morning, and after a while it came back to them. Nick searched their faces as they explored their feelings. He seemed to fade pretty quickly. He found himself yearning to know of their affairs, their successes, the novels and the new ideas that the few who remembered him might say he never knew, he never lived to find out. It was the morning's vision of the empty street, but projected far forward, into afternoons like this one decades hence, in the absent hum of their own business. The emotion was startling. It was a sort of terror, made up of emotions from every stage of his short life, weaning, homesickness, envy and self-pity; but he felt that the self-pity belonged to a larger pity. It was a love of the world that was shockingly unconditional. He stared back at the house, and then turned and drifted on. He looked in bewilderment at number 24, the final house with its regalia of stucco swags and bows. It wasn't just this street corner but the fact of a street corner at all that seemed, in the light of the moment, so beautiful.[6]

There are two notes in that passage that seem to me to contain an implicit acknowledgement of the mysterious sacredness of life. There is Nick's self-pity that seemed to belong to a larger pity and was a love of the world that was shockingly unconditional.

It is the extremity of his condition that has revealed the world to Nick, as if for the first time. It is in this sacred space, the place of revelation and wonder, that religion and art can sometimes conjoin: they both stand astonished before the being of being, the there-ness, this-ness, that-ness of things, the fact that there is something not just nothing, and they respond with wonder because it has concentrated their gaze, caused them to attend, and be present, maybe for the first time:

> It wasn't just this street corner but the fact of a street corner at all that seemed, in the light of the moment, so beautiful.

If you abandon religion's explanatory function, you can sometimes get it back through art that stands astonished before the abyss of nothingness from which such beauty has flowed. The strange thing is that this void, this Nothing or No One, gave us birth, and it is impossible not to be emotionally involved with a parent, however absent and indifferent. We find this agonised astonishment in the poems of Paul Celan. I am thinking particularly of 'Psalm'. Celan was a poet of the abyss, a victim of the brutal indifference of history. His parents were lost in the Nazi death camps and he himself, like other Holocaust survivors, committed suicide. He wrote a wrenching series of poems called 'Die Niemandsrose', – 'The No One's Rose'. This is one of them:

ON REFLECTION

No one moulds us again out of earth and clay,
   no one conjures our dust.
No one.

Praised be your name, no one.
For your sake
we shall flower.
Towards
you.

A nothing
we were, are, shall
remain, flowering:
the nothing-, the
no-one's-rose.

With
our pistil soul-bright,
our stamen heaven-ravaged,
our corolla red
with the crimson word which we sang
over, O over
the thorn.[7]

The thorn wound over which we sing is perplexity at our own being, which we cling to as a mysterious gift, but who are we to praise for the gift? The world itself, wherever it came from, as described by the Polish writer Adam Zagajewski, only the mutilated world.

THE MUTILATED WORLD

Try to praise the mutilated world.
Remember June's long days,
and wild strawberries, drops of rosé wine, the dew.
The nettles that methodically overgrow
the abandoned homesteads of exiles.
You must praise the mutilated world.
You watched the stylish yachts and ships;
one of them had a long trip ahead of it,
while salty oblivion awaited others.
You've seen the refugees heading nowhere,
you've heard the executioners sing joyfully.
You should praise the mutilated world.
Remember the moments when we were together
in a white room and the curtain fluttered.
Return in thought to the concert where music flared.
You gathered acorns in the park in autumn
and leaves eddied over the earth's scars.
Praise the mutilated world
and the grey feather a thrush lost,
and the gentle light that strays and vanishes
and returns.[8]

Yes: that's what we can do; even if we can provide no confident answers to Gauguin's questions, we can at least praise the mutilated world that prompted them.

16

A SECULAR SOCIETY

J.M. Coetzee begins his novel *Diary of a Bad Year* with a sceptical meditation on the formation of the state. These are the novel's opening words:

> Every account of the origins of the state starts from the premise that 'we' – not we the readers but some generic we so wide as to exclude no one – participate in its coming into being. But the fact is that the only 'we' we know – ourselves and the people close to us – are born into the state; and our forebears too were born into the state as far back as we can trace. The state is always there before us.[1]

Then he quotes Thomas Hobbes, one of the classic thinkers on the origin of the state, who saw it as a contract we enacted in order to protect ourselves from ourselves:

> . . . outside the commonwealth is the empire of the passions, war, fear, poverty, nastiness, solitude, barbarity, ignorance, savagery; within the commonwealth is the empire of reason, peace, security, wealth, splendour, society, good taste, the sciences and good will.[2]

Commenting on this passage, Coetzee writes:

> What the Hobbesian myth of origins does not mention is that the handover of power to the state is irreversible. The option is not open to us to change our minds, to decide that the monopoly on the exercise of force held by the state, codified in the law, is not what we wanted after all, that we would prefer to go back to a state of nature. We are born subject. From the moment of our birth we are subject.[3]

Another thinker who, like Hobbes, believed in the necessity of the state to control human savagery was Sigmund Freud. Here he is in *Civilization and Its Discontents*:

> Human life in common is only made possible when a majority comes together which is stronger than any separate individual and which remains united against all separate individuals. The power of this community is then set up as 'right' in opposition to the power of the individual, which is condemned as 'brute force'. This replacement of the power of the individual by the power of the community constitutes the decisive step of civilization.[4]

In another essay, 'The Future of an Illusion', Freud discusses what would happen if we abandoned the social contract and returned to the state of nature. He writes:

> What would then remain would be a state of nature, and that would be far harder to bear. It is true that

> nature would not demand any restrictions of instinct from us, she would let us do as we liked; but she has her own particularly effective method of restricting us. She destroys us – coldly, cruelly, relentlessly, as it seems to us, and possibly through the very things that occasioned our satisfaction. It was precisely because of these dangers with which nature threatens us that we came together and created civilization, which is also, among other things, intended to make our communal life possible. For the principal task of civilization, its actual raison d'être, is to defend us against nature.[5]

I've no idea whether Coetzee ever commented on these words of Freud, but it is not hard to imagine what he might have said. He would have pointed out that the trouble with civilisation or the state or the commonwealth – to give it its various labels – is that it is not exempt from the human vices it was invented to discipline and control. In fact, it can concentrate and amplify them so horribly that we end up in a state far worse than anything we observe in nature itself.

An insight into how this happens is found in another book. In *The Philosopher and the Wolf* Mark Rowlands describes how a wolf he adopted dominated his life till its death ten years later, and prompted him to reflect on the difference between the simian and lupine personalities, the contrast between apes and wolves. *We* are apes, the most intelligent of an intelligent species, top of the simian chain. At some point apes took an evolutionary turn that wolves did not and became social animals – which may even be the source of the myth of the social contract. Rowlands observes that while living in groups shapes the capacity to develop protective alliances, it also shapes the ability to scheme and deceive. Indeed, scheming and deception seem to be at the core of the type of intelligence that developed in apes and reached its apotheosis in *homo sapiens*, the king of the apes. Apes are intuitively political. Wolves never went down this path. In the wolf pack there is little scheming and deception; little, if any, premeditation: life is lived in the urgent primacy of the now. Because of the kind of intelligence that evolved in the human ape, we can do things that wolves could never dream of. We can create art and establish complex social, religious and political institutions, but the shadow cast by this brilliance is our capacity for deception, conspiracy, complexity and cruelty, especially when we are operating at the collective level. The American theologian Reinhold Niebuhr wrote a book called *Moral Man and Immoral Society*, to remind us of the viciousness and cruelty we are capable of when we become a mob, and to show us how the mentality of the mob can take over a state. That is why we should maintain a profound suspicion towards the state and an enduring scepticism about its claim to be our protector. There are too many examples of the state lynching powerless individuals in the name of a higher purpose that turns out to be a great evil.

Let me recall an example from the anti-Apartheid struggles of the 1960s. There was a South African boxer called Ronnie van der Walt, who was the golden boy of white boxing fans in what was then a racist state. He had knocked out a contender for the world welter-weight title and seemed to be on his way to boxing glory. One night, just before he was to fight another white boxer, his name was inked out of the programme and his picture was stripped from the walls. Had he fought that night he would have gone to jail. His boxing career was over, because the South African government had reclassified him as coloured and banned him from fighting white men in the ring. As Ronnie remembered it, 'The inspector walked around us peering at us from every angle like you do when you buy an animal. He said nothing, just looked.' Soon Ronnie got a letter telling him that at 29 he had been reclassified as coloured. That meant he could no longer box for a living, live in a white neighbourhood or send his children to a white school. The state had pulled up his life like a weed from the roadside, and protesting was useless. After pointing out that he was the grandson of Johannes van der Welt, a great Afrikaans wrestler, he added. 'They can't just cut me down like a bloody tree. For God's sake, I am a man.' Those words express the experience of millions of ordinary, unknown individuals down the years who have been sacrificed by the state's addiction to control and separation. Here is another example, this one closer to home.

Until 1967 in England and 1980 in Scotland, it was a criminal offence for a man to have sex with another man, and the full power of the law was visited upon anyone who dared break the law. Our so-called free and democratic state destroyed the lives of thousands of gay men and cut them down like trees. Here is a single example from the crowded annals of the homophobic British state. Alan Turing was a brilliant mathematician and pioneer of computer science. During the Second World War he worked at the Government Code and Cypher School at

Bletchley Park, where he helped to break the German naval ciphers — the famous Enigma Code — and thereby helped to shorten the war. Turing, who was gay, was arrested in 1952 and charged with a criminal sexual offence. The judge gave him the option of going to prison or being chemically castrated with injections of female hormones. He opted for chemical castration, but the effects were so devastating and undermining that rather than go on living with the humiliation he committed suicide in 1954.

All states arrogate to themselves the right to cut down individuals like that if it suits them. The thing to notice about this arrogance of power is that, while the state has always been happy to impose its dictates by force, it has also sought to justify them with theory, including religious theory. What I want to do in the rest of this essay is recall the Christian religion's record for supplying transcendental justification for laws and customs we now reject as evil. At the root of Christianity's complicity in the evils of the state lies a pessimistic theology of authority. Here's Freud again:

> Human life in common is only made possible when a majority comes together which is stronger than any separate individual and which remains united against all separate individuals. The power of this community is then set up as 'right' in opposition to the power of the individual, which is condemned as 'brute force'.[6]

Here's how Saint Paul put it:

> Let every soul be subject unto the higher powers. For there is no power but of God: the powers that be are

ordained of God. Whosoever therefore resisteth the power, resisteth the ordinance of God: and they that resist shall receive damnation to themselves. For rulers are not a terror to good works . . . but if thou do that which is evil, be áfraid; for he beareth not the sword in vain: for he is the minister of God, a revenger to execute wrath upon him that doeth evil.

— Romans, 13:1–4

He is the minister of God, a revenger to execute wrath upon him that doeth evil. What is troubling to anyone who knows about the history of religion is the way the wrath of God has been executed on people once defined as evil, whom we would now define as good. Even more troubling is the way religion has been used to sanctify as good institutions we would now define as evil, such as slavery and the racist theory that justified it. In his Edinburgh Gifford Lectures of 2012, published as a book called *Silence: A Christian History,* the historian Diarmaid MacCulloch describes the origins of a racist theory that is still current in parts of the USA. It is based on the story of the temptation of Eve by the serpent in Genesis.

Now the serpent was more subtil than any beast of the field which the Lord God had made. And he saith unto the woman, Yea, hath God said, Ye shall not eat of every tree of the garden? . . . God doth know that in the day ye eat thereof, then your eyes shall be opened, and ye shall be as gods, knowing good and evil.

— Genesis, 3:1–5

Before looking at the racist spin that was later put on this story, it is worth reminding ourselves that for centuries it was also used to justify the oppression of women. Adam blamed Eve when God discovered that the original couple had eaten the forbidden fruit: 'The woman gave me and I did eat,' he moaned, laying the blame for all subsequent human misery on woman. And from the language of that ancient myth was spun a whole theory of the danger of woman to male rectitude. This is a fourth-century saint on the subject:

> What else is woman but a foe to friendship, an inescapable punishment, a necessary evil, a natural temptation, a desirable calamity, a domestic danger, a delectable detriment, an evil painted with faint colours![7]

With a psychic virus like that lurking in its DNA, it is no surprise that Christianity took so long to emancipate women, an emancipation that has still not occurred in the biggest Christian institution on the planet, the Roman Catholic church; nor in Islamic regimes in Persia and the Middle East.

But let me get back to racism and that serpent. In 1810 a Methodist scholar called Adam Clarke wondered if the serpent – *nachash* in Hebrew – might not have been some kind of ape. This entirely groundless speculation provoked the scorn of serious biblical scholars, but it was grabbed by racists in the USA who went on to identify the Negro with the ape in the frame. MacCulloch comments:

> In the age of Charles Darwin, some American defenders of Negro slavery saw it as potentially offering a . . . scientific and respectable and cogent explanation of Negro origins . . . In effect, since the Negro was not fully human, there was no slavery of human beings in the South, and abolitionists were wasting their breath.[8]

But slave holders did not have to rely on the Old Testament alone for support for their cause – the New Testament did an even better job for them. Here's MacCulloch again:

> The distressing fact for modern Christians . . . is that slavery is taken for granted in the Bible, even if it is not always considered to be a good thing, at least for oneself. One would have had to be exceptionally independent-minded and intellectually awkward to face up to the consensus of every philosopher in the ancient world, and the first Christians did not rise to the challenge. Paul's Epistle to Philemon, in which the Apostle asks his correspondent to allow him the continued services of Philemon's slave Onesimus, is a Christian foundation document in the justification of slavery.[9]

So, who first found the courage to challenge the authority of the Bible and denounce slavery as evil? MacCulloch names Pennsylvanian Quakers of 1688 as the first in the game. And what is significant is how they went about it. MacCulloch again:

> Quakers . . . believed in the prime authority of the 'inner light'. Many of their earliest activists . . . had through

their sharp critique of the problems of the scriptural text, pioneered the modern Enlightenment discipline of biblical criticism . . . The Quakers' disrespect for the established conventions of biblical authority was the reason that they could take a fresh perspective on biblical authority and reject it. It took original minds to kick against the authority of sacred Scriptures. What was needed was a prior conviction in one's conscience of the wrongness of slavery, which one might then decide to justify by a purposeful re-examination of the Bible.[10]

What was needed was a prior conviction in one's conscience of the wrongness of slavery . . . Savour those words for a moment to grasp the importance of what had happened. The problem with basing morality on an ancient text revealed by God as an enduring guide to conduct is that it locks us into the social and scientific world-view of the time of its provenance. The reason it has been so hard for Christianity to ditch attitudes that secular society thinks are antediluvian is that they have been seen not as the dated arrangements of Bronze Age society, but as eternal norms. That is why we admire the courage of those Pennsylvanian Quakers who knew the difference between what was right and what the Bible once said was right. For them slavery was wrong even if the Bible appeared to justify it, the implication being that the Bible was a human not a divine creation. This was the kind of insight that had led to the Enlightenment in the eighteenth century, when light bulbs switched on in people's heads and they looked at religion's sacred books and said to themselves, why should we bind ourselves to what these ancient texts tell us when our own sense of justice is outraged by what they say? Let me gather these strands together and offer a conclusion.

We humans have organised ourselves into states or commonwealths in order to control our own unruly passions and bring some stability to our affairs; but the systems we created in the past reflected our vices as well as our virtues, and they entrenched social arrangements from distant times, many of them intensely cruel. Moral evolution is hard enough at any time, but religion adds to the difficulty by anointing these volatile social arrangements with the absolute authority of God. That is why in societies where religious institutions are powerful, social change is strongly resisted. If you have been persuaded by your religion that humanity's social arrangements are not historically contingent but were preordained by God to last for ever, then how can you be persuaded to change your mind about them? Gay marriage – to take a current example that obsesses the Anglican Communion – is not a matter of widening access to a human institution that has fluctuated in meaning and observance, it is to challenge an order eternally fixed by God.

That is why, as the pace of social change quickens, we should reassert the founding principle of the secular state and claim it anew. In the name of that principle, we will continue to extend toleration towards institutions that are themselves intolerant; but we will not permit them to export their institutional prejudices into the secular sphere. They may continue to discriminate against women and gays in the sanctuary; but we will not permit them to do so in the public square. However, our adherence to the secular spirit must include a strong admixture of scepticism towards the secular state itself. Central to my thesis in this essay is that the human animal, this clever ape, is easily corrupted by power and inevitably misuses it. Secular powers are not exempt from this weakness, which is why we must build round them a system of checks, balances and reversals.

There are two types of people who are fundamental to this process of constant challenge to the corruptions of institutional power: the victim and the dissident. It is victims who guarantee moral progress in society by organising opposition to the powers that oppress them, and their allies are outsiders who are constitutionally incapable of buying permanently into any system. Combined, these two groups act as creative destabilisers of institutional power in all its forms. Marx said this was done not by the weakening of the strong but by the strengthening of the weak. This was how slavery was abolished and women emancipated and gay people liberated.

I began this essay by agreeing with the opening words of J.M. Coetzee's novel *Diary of a Bad Year*. I want to end by disagreeing with his closing words, when he writes:

> If I were to give my brand of political thought a label, I would call it pessimistic anarchistic quietism, or anarchistic quietistic pessimism, or pessimistic quietistic anarchism: anarchism because experience tells me that what is wrong with politics is power itself; quietism because I have my doubts about the will to set about changing the world, a will infected with the drive to

power; and pessimism because I am sceptical that, in a fundamental way, things can be changed.[11]

I would change one word in Coetzee's self-description and commend a political stance called pessimistic anarchistic *activism*. Pessimistic, because it is obvious that the human ape is a cruel and tricky customer we shouldn't trust with too much power; anarchistic, because it is obvious that power corrupts those who hold it and the institutions they create; but *activism* not *quietism,* because history proves that the world can be changed. If change were not possible, we would still have slavery, and the oppression of women, and gay men stoned to death as the Bible dictates. We ended all these abuses, in spite of the opposition of religious institutions, so we should continue to watch them with a wary eye. You are welcome to remain part of our society, we should tell them, but keep your prejudices under your own steeples.

17

DARWIN AND THE BIBLE

People who enjoyed a good punch-up relished what happened in 2009, when we celebrated the 150th anniversary of the publication of Charles Darwin's, *The Origin of Species*. One way to characterise the event was to see it as the Battle of the Books, a confrontation between two sacred texts and their priestly guardians. On the one hand there was the Bible, inspired by God three thousand and so years ago; and on the other hand, there was Darwin's revolutionary study that made the claims of the Bible look absurd, and precipitated an unnecessary crisis of faith for those who had been taught to read them literally not mythically. If you listen to the extremists in this continuing debate, you get the impression that that's still the choice, when, in fact, the debate is much more interesting and complex than that. One of the difficulties is that while there may be only one way of reading *The Origin of Species*, there are many ways of reading the Bible, and it is the Bible I mainly want to think about in this essay.

Among believers, the Bible is held either to have been personally dictated by God or to contain words directly inspired by God. If we ask on what authority these claims are made, we are told that it is the Bible itself that makes them. It is easy to mock this kind of circularity, and no one did it more scathingly than an eighteenth-century theologian called Matthew Tindal:

> It is an odd jumble to prove the truth of a book by the truth of the doctrines it contains, and at the same time conclude these doctrines to be true because contained in that book.[1]

It is the circularity of religious argument that accounts for the frustration many feel when they encounter believers who argue a case, not on its merits, but on the authority of the Bible.

This is a frustration experienced by believers themselves, as the debate between creationists and evolutionists demonstrates. On the basis of the self-authenticating authority of the Bible, creationists assert that the world and its inhabitants were fully established in six days, roughly seven thousand years ago.

> And God saw everything that he had made, and, behold, it was very good. And the evening and the morning were the sixth day. Thus the heavens and the earth were finished, and all the host of them. And on the seventh day God ended his work which he had made; and he rested on the seventh day from all his work which he had made.
>
> — Genesis, 1:31; 2:1–2

Evolutionists, convinced by Darwin's researches, assert that living species on earth emerged over an unimaginably long period of time by a process of experimental adaptation, so the claims of the Bible are risible. There is a mediating position between the opposed protagonists, sometimes called 'intelligent design'. Those who take this line agree with creationists about the existence of an ultimate Designer, but they think that its method of operating was the one discovered by Darwin. For them the world is the way science describes it, except for the single claim that it is ultimately the work of God.

The intriguing thing about this debate is that it shows that even within the community of believers, there are different ways of reading the Bible. Some give it an absolute suprahistorical authority. If you read the Bible from this perspective, it locks you permanently into the world view of texts that reached their final form over 2,000 years ago. We only have to think about the revolution that has occurred in the status of women, the subject of a previous essay, to see how difficult it must be to maintain this kind of belief in the authority of the Bible, while respecting society's current ethical imperatives, not to mention the extraordinary advances in the scientific understanding of nature. That is why a more subtle and flexible approach to scripture emerged among thinkers within the believing community itself. For them, all history, including the history of the Bible, is a gradual process of divine disclosure that is commensurate with human rationality and its discoveries. Applying this principle to the Bible means you can accept an entirely naturalistic account of its history, but with the proviso that its ultimate, originating authority is God. Like the world, the Bible is seen as the work of God, but its nature and meaning are disclosed to us by the application of the tools of historical and scientific research. That is why, while some Christians prefer to read the Bible in a literalistic way, others come at its meaning more circuitously; it just depends on the kind of believers they are.

But those two positions do not exhaust our options. There is another way of understanding the Bible, and to explain it I'll offer a triangulation approach to biblical interpretation. Just as a triangle has three angles, so there are three ways of using the Bible: two for believers, and one for everyone else. I have already covered the views from the believing base of the triangle: the angle from the right that takes the Bible as literal dictation from God; and the angle from the left that takes it as a human construct, though one inspired by God. Though they come to very different conclusions about it, both of these approaches accord extrinsic authority to the Bible – its value comes from outside itself.

Let us look now at the third angle of the triangle, and bring in the ancient Greeks to assist us. The Greeks employed a distinction in their use of language. They used the word *logos* for factual discourse about things that could be verified through the senses; but they used the word *muthos* to describe another kind of meaning. The most characteristic use of this word was to classify stories about the gods, which is why it is easily misunderstood today. The word myth has become synonymous with something false or untrue, but the question we should ask of a myth is not whether it is true or false, but whether it is living or dead, whether it still carries meaning for us today.

When Sigmund Freud was exploring the mysteries of

human nature, he borrowed from Greek mythology to express his discoveries. An example is his theory of what he called the Oedipus complex. In the Greek myth, Oedipus was the son of the King and Queen of Thebes. To avert the prophecy that he would one day kill his father and marry his mother, he was exposed on the mountains as an infant. Rescued and reared by shepherds, and unaware of his lineage, when he grew to manhood Oedipus unwittingly killed his father and married his mother. Freud uses this myth to explain his psychoanalytic term for a son's unacknowledged sexual desire for his mother and hatred of his father. What Freud gives us here is not factual science; it is myth. That is why when we read him, we grasp the truth of his insights experientially rather than theoretically. As with these old myths, much of what he writes corresponds to the way we encounter the tumult of our own minds. That is why he is better understood as a therapeutic artist or priest than as a scientist; and it is why he is often wilfully misunderstood by rigorously empirical thinkers.

And that is what has happened to the Bible itself: unimaginative literalists have destroyed its reputation by insisting on the factual truth of the myth of the Fall in Genesis, rather than encouraging us to read it as a metaphor for the enduring human capacity for self-destruction. Reading the Bible through the lens of myth can be illuminating, even for non-believers. For readers who follow this approach, the Bible has intrinsic not extrinsic authority; it carries the power of its meaning within itself, like any great text. It is significant that one of the communities most aware of the power of sacred texts to help humanity in its search for emotional wellbeing is the psychotherapeutic profession. Those who work with military veterans suffering from post-traumatic stress disorder sometimes use the epics of Homer and the dramas of Euripides to help them uncover and articulate their own traumas. That is what religious practitioners at their best have always done with their sacred texts. They have used them to help us understand ourselves and change for the better. This way of reading the Bible need not be discontinuous with the interpretation offered by believers. Just as believers can accept the way science sees the world, though they believe God is its final author, so they can accept the way therapists read the Bible, though they believe God is its final author.

And for those who can't figure out what side they are on, let me end with a poem by Norman MacCaig:

A MAN I AGREED WITH

He knew better than to admire a chair
and say *What does it mean?*

He loved everything that accepted
the unfailing hospitality of his five senses.
He would say *Hello, caterpillar* or
So long, Loch Fewin.

He wanted to know
how they came to be what they are:
But he never insulted them by saying
Caterpillar, Loch Fewin, what do you mean?

DARWIN AND THE BIBLE

In this respect he was like God,
though he was godless. — He knew the difference
Between *What does it mean to me?*
And *What does it mean?*

That's why he said, half smiling,
Of course, God, like me,
Is an atheist.[2]

18

IMPROVISING ETHICS

The difficulty that many of us face today is that we find ourselves spiritually homeless, because we are no longer comfortably and unselfconsciously established at the heart of any of the great religious traditions. And it is with the nature of tradition itself I want to start. There are a number of formulas that try to capture the atmosphere of our society in these early years of the third millennium, but the one that is the simplest and easiest to expound is 'the end of tradition': ours is a post-traditional society. A tradition is a system of ideas and practices based on a set of assumptions or premises from which a complex social or religious structure has evolved. Let me give you an example of a theological system from the Christian tradition that might help us to understand how these constructs work. Here again are those verses I keep quoting from the Letter to the Romans, Chapter 5, which are, in effect, an early Christian commentary on Genesis, Chapter 3:

> It was through one man that sin entered the world, and through sin death, and thus death pervaded the whole human race, inasmuch as all have sinned. But

God's act of grace is out of all proportion to Adam's wrongdoing. For if the wrongdoing of that one man brought death upon so many, its effect is vastly exceeded by the grace of God and the gift that came to so many by the grace of the one man, Jesus Christ. If, by the wrongdoing of one man, death established its reign through that one man, much more shall those who in far greater measure receive grace and the gift of righteousness live and reign through the one man Jesus Christ. It follows then, that as the result of one misdeed was condemnation for all people, so the result of one righteous act is acquittal and life for all. For as through the disobedience of one man many were made sinners, so through the obedience of one man many will be made righteous.

It would be hard to exaggerate the importance of that passage in the formation of the Christian theological tradition and its effect on human self-understanding down the centuries. Let me pick out a few salient details. Paul takes it for granted that his readers will know the story of Adam and Eve from the Book of Genesis, Chapter 3:1–4.

> Now the serpent was more subtil that any beast of the field which the Lord God had made. And he said unto the woman, Yea, hath God said, Ye shall not eat of every tree of the garden? And the woman said unto the serpent, We may eat of the fruit of the trees of the garden: but of the fruit of the tree which is in the midst of the garden, Ye shall not eat of it, lest ye die. And the serpent said unto the woman, Ye shall not surely die.

But because they do eat of the fruit of the forbidden tree, Paul spells out the consequences – with some very dodgy reasoning.

> It was through one man that sin entered the world, and through sin death, and thus death pervaded the whole human race, inasmuch as all have sinned.

In that statement, Paul makes two important and related claims. The first is that by virtue of having been born, we inherit the guilt of Adam and Eve like a genetic defect; and, as a consequence, we all die.

Now, let now us move forward eighteen hundred years to see how Paul's historicising of that ancient myth has had a continuing impact not only on Christian self-understanding, but on Christian theological development. On 8 December 1854, Pope Pius IX promulgated the dogma of Mary's Immaculate Conception, and that is the date on which the feast is kept in the Roman Catholic church. The dogma states that

> . . . from the first moment of her conception the Blessed Virgin Mary was, by the singular grace and privilege of God, and in view of the merits of Jesus Christ, Saviour of Mankind, kept free from all stain of original sin.[1]

And because Mary was miraculously preserved from original sin and remained without sin throughout her life, she was not subject to the penalty of physical death, described by Saint Paul as the consequence of sin, so she was assumed bodily into heaven, a doctrine that was formally defined by Pope Pius XII in 1950.

> We proclaim and define it to be a dogma revealed by God that the immaculate Mother of God, Mary ever virgin, when the course of her earthly life was finished, was taken up body and soul into the glory of heaven.[2]

Behind both of these Mariological developments there sits the narrative of the Fall in Genesis:

> The Woman whom thou gavest to be with me, she gave me of the tree, and I did eat.
> – Genesis: 3:12

The Christological implications of this ancient narrative were even more profound than the Mariological dogmas they later gave rise to. The first, Adam's disobedience, infected us with guilt; but the second, Adam's obedience and self-sacrifice, intervened mystically to switch off the curse that had condemned us to death. Jesus Christ, whom Paul identifies as the second Adam, becomes the answer to the problem created for the human race by the original disobedience of Adam and Eve, and the punishment of death it had brought on humanity. If you accept the originating assumption, the premise on which the system is based, it works with captivating simplicity. And it has enormous dramatic power. It has profoundly affected the poetry of worship in the Christian tradition, as well as the mechanics of evangelistic preaching. As a working tradition, its echoes are all around us. People who have never read The Book of Genesis or Paul's Letter to the Romans get the cartoon significance of Adam and Eve, the snake, the apple and the fig leaf.

But what happens when you question the premise, the originating assumption, on which the system is built? What happens to a tradition when you no longer believe the historical claim on which it stands? We know that the story of Adam and Eve is a myth, a narrative device for conveying abstract truth. It is not history; it does not account for anything, except its own meaning. We know, for instance, that death is not a punishment for sin, but a biological necessity, an ineluctable fact of life. We experience it as loss. It fills us with fear. We may rage against it, but we know it is not a punishment handed out to the human race because of Adam's disobedience. We also know that without death, life on our little planet would become unbearable. We have already over-heated the planet; without death we would have over-populated it centuries ago, and suffocated ourselves in the process.

> To obviate the absolute necessity of death, the reproduction of living things would have had to cease soon after it began. The consequence of this would be the absence of all growth, the evolution of the species. Man, the result of a long evolutionary process, would never have appeared on earth, or, on the assumption that he was 'created' on the first day of the biosphere, would never have evolved to his present state. In a word, we can conceive of the absence of death only in an entirely static universe where a determined number of members of different species would have been

created in the beginning and remained constant for the duration . . . there is no doubt that in an evolutionary universe death is a necessity.[3]

We also know that, captivating as such myths are, there never was a golden age of human innocence, nor any idyllic Garden of Eden from which our parents were banished because they had disobeyed God's instructions. The myth is still powerful because it expresses the tragedy of the many ways we go on ruining our own happiness, but it is not a historic event on which we can build a sustainable system. Women are not disproportionately responsible for human sinfulness, and their subjection to men was an aspect of patriarchy, not a punishment from God. When we use the Adam and Eve myth today, we do not treat it as history, we do not build arguments on it, we use it as a more-or-less instructive parable of the human condition.

There are religious communities that still use these ancient narratives as if they were fixed and established facts like the multiplication table; but the prevailing intellectual ethos of our society does the opposite. It questions the premises on which all traditional systems are based; and it repudiates the claims of religious revelation to decree infallibly how the rest of us should live. For example, when the tradition, quoting its scripture, tells society that women should be subordinate to men or that same-sex lovers should be condemned, society asks: 'Why?' It wants the reason for the prohibition. And it is here we come to the main difference between the contemporary ethos and traditional religion. Post-traditional society is quite prepared to identify certain kinds of conduct as wrong, but the basis for the wrong has to be demonstrated, reasons have to be given. For instance, it is strongly opposed to abusive sexual relationships, because it believes consent is an important ethical value, whatever the context. Traditional religions operate on the basis of the authority of their claims, not their moral defensibility. That is why when we ask them why same-sex love is wrong they offer us a text rather than an argument, they point to the tradition as though it had no history, they refer to it as if it were beyond interpretation. Here's that quotation from Matthew Tindal again.

> It is an odd jumble to prove the truth of a book by the truth of the doctrines it contains, and at the same time conclude these doctrines to be true because contained in that book.

Let me return for a few minutes to my opening claim that the best way to understand much of what is going on in our society is to see it as at the end of tradition, or post-traditional. This is a complex phenomenon, but it seems to have been produced by a number of elements, the most important of which is *globalisation*. We are familiar with this term as a description of the economic system that dominates the world. It is called the global market economy and, whatever we think of it, we all have to acknowledge that it has bonded the world together in a way that has shrunk distance. A crisis in Tokyo or Jakarta will have immediate effects in London or New York. We are now familiar with the idea of the world as a global village, but it is a mistake to limit this metaphor to the economic system. It has profoundly affected the religious and intellectual currencies of the world, as well as its economic systems.

Apart from anything else that might be said about them, we are now aware of other systems and traditions, other paradigms, using that term to mean 'an entire constellation of beliefs, values, techniques which are shared by the members of a particular community', to quote Thomas Kuhn, author of *The Structure of Scientific Revolutions* in 1962, and the originator of paradigm theory. We have got so used to this kind of liberal recognition of the claims of other human systems that we easily forget how new it is. Paradigms or traditions operate at their best when we are completely unaware that we are in one. *Our* paradigm is not an arbitrary human construct, the way we happen to do things; it is the way things actually are. This is why, for instance, when the European colonists encountered the very different paradigms or world views held by the native peoples in North, Central or South America, they dismissed them as primitive, devilish and without value. This spiritual arrogance and lack of imagination was the prelude to the horrifying genocide and destruction of ancient cultures that characterised European colonisation in the Americas as well as in Australia. The irony is that today, in our own spiritually dehydrated landscape, some are turning back to the cultures their forebears tried to eradicate, because they contain enduring wisdom, not least in their attitude to the earth and their reverence for creation.

Globalisation makes it impossible for us to be unaware of other traditions, other ways of looking at the world. The resulting shift in attitude is what we call pluralism.

Indeed, 'plural society' rather than 'post-traditional society' might be a more accurate description of our situation today. In many ways, ours is a multi-traditional society, but the experience of encountering other cultures and other paradigms has an eroding effect on the way in which any tradition is held. The term that describes this process of cultural erosion is 'relativism', and there are two subtly different meanings to the term. One is descriptive: as a matter of fact, it says, your tradition or cultural paradigm is usually relative to your context and its inherited perspectives. If you were born in the Republic of Ireland the chances are that you'll be a Catholic; if you were born in Turkey the chances are that you'll be a Muslim; if you were born in India the chances are that you'll be a Hindu. A subtler form of relativism would claim that the points of view themselves are all relative, and there is no way we can say that any one of them is superior to any other. I shall want to challenge that view, but it is important to recognise that one of the inescapable aspects of our multi- or post-traditional society is that it generates an awareness that there are many human cultures and value systems, an awareness that has an inevitably relativising effect.

Many people find that this kind of society induces enormous anxiety, because it has shifted all the landmarks that once guided us and made us feel that we knew where we were. So let me look now at some of the responses to the situation we are in. One of the most fascinating of the three responses I want to look at is 'fundamentalism'. The British sociologist Anthony Giddens defined fundamentalism as 'defending tradition in the traditional way'. The fundamentalist refers to ancient assumptions as if they were valid for all time and require no new justification or adaptation. In periods of accelerating social change, fundamentalism is a refuge for many. Its refusal to negotiate with the new consciousness is its greatest strength, but for those of us who find ourselves within the new consciousness, its insistence on cleaving to the original meaning of ancient traditions renders them inaccessible to us, because it places them beyond any kind of negotiation.

For example, as far as the tradition we looked at earlier goes, the fundamentalist would simply state that the Adam and Eve story is a historic event and Paul's exposition of it is true: death is the wages of sin; the woman did fall for the tempter; and everyone is born guilty of an aboriginal offence committed by our primal parents. Jesus Christ's mission was to rescue us from the destiny forged for us by the sin of Adam, by substituting himself for us in the sacrifice God demanded in atonement and reparation, and dying to save us from our sins. When you engage in dialogue with fundamentalists you soon discover that no real negotiation or exchange is possible. Fundamentalism is one of the most dangerously volatile elements in our world, ranging from the wilder reaches of the Christian Right in the USA to the violent excesses of Muslim fundamentalists in the Middle East.

The philosopher Isaiah Berlin was one of the best interpreters of the tragically plural nature of human values. He warned us that the dilemmas that confront us are just as likely to be between opposing or what he called incommensurable or irreconcilable goods, as between an obvious good and an obvious evil. To recognise this is finally to understand the tragic nature of many of our choices, even of life itself. He wrote:

> If we are not armed with an a priori guarantee of the proposition that a total harmony of true values is somewhere to be found, we must fall back on the ordinary resources of empirical observation and ordinary human knowledge. And these certainly give us no warrant for supposing that all good things, or all bad things for that matter, are reconcilable with each other. The world that we encounter in ordinary experience is one in which we are faced with choices between ends equally ultimate, and claims equally absolute, the realisation of some of which must inevitably involve the sacrifice of others. Indeed, it is because this is their situation that men place such immense value upon the freedom to choose; for if they had assurance that in some perfect state, realisable by men on earth, no ends pursued by them would ever be in conflict, the necessity and agony of choice would disappear, and with it the central importance of the freedom to choose. Any method of bringing this final state nearer would then seem fully justified, no matter how much freedom were sacrificed to forward its advance.
>
> It is, I have no doubt, some such dogmatic certainty that has been responsible for the deep, serene, unshakeable conviction in the minds of some of the most merciless tyrants and persecutors in history that what they did was fully justified by its purpose . . . If, as I believe, the ends of men are many, and not all of them are in principle compatible with each other, then the possibility of conflict – and of tragedy – can never wholly be eliminated from

human life, either personal or social. The necessity of choosing between absolute claims is then an inescapable characteristic of the human condition.[4]

We might summarise Isaiah Berlin's account of moral pluralism in this way: it is a rejection of the idea of a perfect religion or society or family. Life is manifold in the forms it takes; it is gloriously and inescapably plural. So, we are in the business of making trade-offs between conflicting goods, and there is no infallible measuring system for weighing these values against each other. That is why we often reach situations where further reflective deliberation gets us no further and we have no choice but to act.[5] I am reminded of a famous politician's statement that in politics one never reaches conclusions, but one must sometimes make decisions.[6]

What all this means in practical terms is that we must achieve a considerable level of magnanimity towards other people as moral agents, especially if they are working within very different systems to our own. We will find that in the moral life tragic choices between different goods have to be made and it is wise not to try to iron everything into an unachievable unified world view. A fundamental moral value in our time is the ability to tolerate systems that we would not choose for ourselves. This value of tolerance is a difficult one for passionately single-minded adherents of exclusive moral traditions to achieve, but it is an important value for society as a whole, even if it is one that particular moral communities within the larger community do not themselves value highly.

Though most of the conflicts we engage in are between

opposing goods, conflicting values, rather than between a straight right and an obvious wrong, this does not mean that we will refuse to take a stand, make a decision or choose one of the options in a particular conflict. But it ought to moderate our appetite for dismissing those who are opposed to us on the grounds that they are immoral or have no values. Managing these intractable disagreements in a plural culture is difficult. Most of us probably feel that somewhere beyond argument there is a unified theory of human nature and its values and that, if we struggle hard enough, we'll find it. Both experience and reflection contradict that. This, however, is not moral relativism. It is not saying that one attitude is no better or worse than any other. To say that values conflict is not to say that there are no values at all, no fundamental principles that characterise us as human. Our tragedy is not that we are indifferent to the good, but that we recognise that it is sometimes in conflict with itself. Berlin is quite clear that pluralism of the sort he describes is not the same thing as moral relativism:

> ... if I find a man to whom it literally makes no difference whether he kicks a pebble or kills his family ... I shall not be disposed, like consistent relativists, to attribute to him merely a different code of morality from my own or that of most men, but shall begin to speak of insanity and inhumanity; I shall be inclined to consider him mad; which is a way of saying that I do not regard such a being as being fully a man at all.[7]

Berlin's distinction between the absence of values and the

fact that genuine values can be in conflict with one another will be fundamental if we are not to be immobilised from the work of moral reconstruction by the confusions of our time. In that work, we will have to recognise the importance of consent by men and women to the moral projects they are invited to enter. But we will also have to recognise that the same men and women are capable of making different choices on perfectly valid grounds, so considerable magnanimity will be required of us, if we are to live peaceably in plural moral communities. This is not the same thing as saying anything goes or that there are no universal moral principles. Improvising ethics is taxing, but it can also be exhilarating!

19

HAS FAITH A FUTURE?

I want to begin with a quote from Rick Hertzberg, who used to write the 'Talk of the Town' columns in the *New Yorker*. He wrote the piece during the second term of the Reagan administration, provoked by William Bennett, Reagan's Secretary for Education; a man who, it was later revealed, had frittered away millions of dollars in the gambling dens of Las Vegas and Atlantic City. Bennett had complained that the people who really ruled the country – the liberals, the judges, the whatever – had consistently displayed a disdain for the Judeo-Christian values that had made America great. Hertzberg, son of an unbelieving Jewish father and a Quaker mother, fired off this reply:

> As a Judeo-Christian who has an aversion to religion, and who is an American as good as or better than any mousse-haired, Bible-touting, apartheid-promoting evangelist on any UHF television station you can name, I must protest.
> Where was it written that if you don't like religion you are somehow disqualified from being a legitimate American? What was Mark Twain, a Russian? When did

it become un-American to have opinions about the origin and meaning of the universe that come from sources other than the body of dogma of organizations approved by the federal government as certifiably Judeo-Christian? If it is American to believe that God ordered Tribe X to abjure pork, or that he caused Leader Y to be born to a virgin, why is it suddenly un-American to doubt that the prime mover of this unimaginably vast universe of quintillions of solar systems would be likely to be obsessed with questions involving the dietary and sexual behaviour of a few thousand bipeds inhabiting a small part of a speck of dust orbiting a third-rate star in an obscure spiral arm of one of a million of more or less identical galaxies?[1]

I offer two words in response. My first word is *Amen*. Amen because, like Rick Hertzberg, I object to the way some religious leaders privilege their sacred texts above all other texts on earth as carriers of knowledge and wisdom. But 'nevertheless' is my second word, because it is by means of the frail biped *homo sapiens*, inhabiting that small part of a speck of dust orbiting a third-rate star in an obscure spiral arm of one of a million of more or less identical galaxies that this universe of quintillions of solar systems is now thinking about itself and has become aware of its own existence.

There may be self-conscious, thinking creatures in other corners of the universe, but we are the only ones we know about, and it is worth savouring the fact. In us, and maybe only in us, the universe is thinking about itself and wondering where it came from, and it seems to have taken fourteen billion years to produce us. That is why Ludwig Wittgenstein said it is not 'WHAT the world is, but THAT it is, which is the mystical'. Given the fundamental uncertainty of all that, I am intrigued by the similarities between confident theists and equally confident atheists, and their psychological interchangeability. I belong in neither camp, but my agnosticism is not a weak, vacillating neutrality, it is a commitment to staying in a place of passionate and curious uncertainty. That said, I value the existence of both these opposing certainties, though I cannot commit myself exclusively to either of them. I value the poetry of belief, its myths and narratives, its longing for meaning and the way it has turned that longing into beauty in word and music. I want that kept around, purged of arrogance and cruelty, weakened and less certain, but still there.

I also value the purging critical role of unbelief and the way it cuts through the cruel certainties of religion, most of which have come down to us from Bronze Age cultures. I love the way unbelief challenges the scientific ignorance of reactionary belief, and I especially love the way it has stretched and aged this astonishing universe in which we are set.

And yet, there is something about both of these absolutist positions I cannot commit myself to. I don't want the mystery solved and tied up for me, because I have seen too many premature resolutions in human history and I don't like what they can do to people. That is why I keep coming back to Louis MacNeice and his passion for expectancy and surprise. Don't be too sure you know what's going on, but be ready for surprises, is his advice:

HAS FAITH A FUTURE?

If there has been no spiritual change of kind
Within our species since Cro-Magnon Man
And none is looked for now while the millennia cool,
Yet each of us has known mutations in the mind
When the world jumped and what had been a plan
Dissolved and rivers gushed from what had seemed a pool.

For every static world that you or I impose
Upon the real one must crack at times and new
Patterns from new disorders open like a rose
And old assumptions yield to new sensation;
The Stranger in the wings is waiting for his cue,
The fuse is always laid to some annunciation.[2]

Faith can have a future, as long as we let it be *faith* and not claim it as *certainty*. It's a bet, a gamble, but with a difference. Blaise Pascal said it was a bet in which, if we win, we win everything; and if we lose, we lose nothing.

20

ARE CHRISTIANS ALLOWED TO BE GAY?

Napier University in Edinburgh has a widely scattered series of campuses, but its main administration block is in a giant Italian villa a couple of miles south of Princes Street. The building was opened in 1880 as the Craiglockhart Hydropathic Institution. It occupies a magnificent site and its central tower commands one of the best views in Scotland, looking away over the Firth of Forth to the distant mountains of Perthshire. The original facilities had included Turkish and swimming baths, and 'ladies' and gentlemen's special bath-rooms, with all the varieties of hot and cold plunge, vapour, spray, needle, douche and electrical baths, with special galvanic apparatus'. In spite of these impressive amenities the place had never prospered and in 1916 it was taken over by the Army for officers suffering from shell shock. If it had not existed, some of the best poetry in the English language would never have been written.

In July 1917 an army officer who was already a well-known poet, Siegfried Sassoon, published 'A Soldier's Declaration':

> I am making this statement as an act of wilful defiance

of military authority, because I believe the war is being deliberately prolonged by those who have the power to end it.

Afraid that his friend would be court martialled, Robert Graves fixed it with the army for Sassoon to be sent to Craiglockhart, where he was treated by the remarkable army psychologist W.H.R. Rivers. Though he never retracted his statement, Sassoon went back to active service in France, because he felt that his work was now to tell the world through his poetry what the war was really like. The whole episode was fictionalised in Pat Barker's novel, *Regeneration*, which was later turned into a fine movie. In 1917 Sassoon was already a mature poet with an authentic voice. The same could hardly be said for Wilfred Owen, whom he met at Craiglockhart that summer.

Owen was born in 1893 in Shropshire, where his father was a railway worker. He had always wanted to go to university and become an educated man, but Shrewsbury Technical School was all his family could afford, and he was always a bit self-conscious about his modest background and provincial accent. Beneath the diffidence, however, there was a formidable human being who emerged to be the greatest of England's World War I poets.

After a period assisting in a country parish (he had contemplated ordination at one time), Owen left in 1913 to teach English in Bordeaux and returned in 1915 to join the army. He was commissioned in the Manchester Regiment in 1916, and on 30 December was sent out to the basecamp at Etaples. In March 1917, after days under fire, he fell asleep on a railway embankment, somewhere near Savy Wood, and was blown into the air by a shell, a near-miss that left him helpless, lying close to the dismembered remains of another officer. When he got back to camp people noticed that he was in shock. His commanding officer called his courage into question, but the doctor diagnosed 'neurasthenia' and it was decided that the best place for him would be Craiglockhart War Hospital in Edinburgh. He arrived there in June 1917.

Owen had experimented with verse from an early age and had read widely, but in 1917 his work was still self-consciously poetic, when he took it shyly along the corridor at Craiglockhart to Sassoon. Sassoon, whom he fell for instantly, taught him that poetry was about reality and helped him to see that it was the war he must deal with. Sassoon's friendship and advice released Owen's genius, and the final year of his life gave us the poetry we remember today. In one of his notebooks Owen scribbled a preface to the poems that were not to be published till four years after his death in 1920:

> Above all, this book is not concerned with Poetry.
> The subject of it is War, and the Pity of War.
> The poetry is in the Pity.[1]

The irony of the regime and its purpose at Craiglockhart was brought out well in the film version of Pat Barker's novel. It is the understanding and sympathetic Doctor Rivers, knowing the horror these men had gone through, who cures them, in order to send them back to the front. Though Sassoon and Owen had lost belief in the war, they went back to it willingly, Owen to the front, where he was killed a week before the war ended, shepherding his men through an artillery barrage on the Sambre Canal in November 1918. He is acknowledged today as the most outstanding of the World War I poets, and it is impossible to read his poems, filled as they are with his contempt for those who drove the war on and his compassion for the soldiers who were its victims, without feeling an angry love rise in you. The film made about his time at Craiglockhart provokes a similar anger and love, and I watched it with deep emotion. Most of the anger I felt was against the folly of the ruling ascendancy who sent all those brave young men to 'die as cattle', in Owen's own phrase. But that was only part of my anger; the other part had a different root.

These two men, both brave beyond any possible bravery, both poets who enriched our literature, and one of whom, Owen, was a great poet whose work will endure, were both gay, though theirs was a love that dared not speak its name at the time. Had the establishment that exploited them and sent them to the trenches found out about their true nature, they would have hounded them to another sort of death. Sassoon the warrior scholar gave Owen more than the freedom to be a great poet; he also gave him the courage to accept his own nature; and these two freedoms were almost certainly related. By saying no to the war and yes to himself, Owen's genius was liberated. Sassoon introduced Owen to his London friends, who included Robert Ross, the great Wildean loyalist, and Osbert Sitwell. Through them he got to know Charles Scott-Moncrieff, who fell in love with him, and who was to make use of Owen's experiments with assonance in his own translation of Proust.

After his release from Craiglockhart, Owen trained at Scarborough and Ripon, but his return to duty was punctuated by visits to London to see his new friends, all of whom seem to have recognised his genius as a poet. He had found love, and through that love he had found his work: war and the pity of war. Owen's tender, yet angry love for his men surges through his poetry. It was why he went back to the front a determined soldier. Early in October he won the Military Cross on the Hindenburg line, even though he hated the war and no longer found any virtue in it. Like E.M. Forster, another gay man of genius, his loyalties now were to his friends, not to the great establishments that rob us of our humanity as they seduce us with the blandishments of their approval. Owen died for his friends, not for the ruthless government that sent them into the trenches, and I find in his death and in the great poetry that came before it, an icon or representational symbol of the place of gay and lesbian people in the culture of the Christian Church.

I offer no new arguments to support the liberation of gay people in Church and society – there are none – but let me touch briefly on the old ones before pushing them away. I'll leave aside the ugly facts of fear and prejudice that add such a destructively unconscious energy to the arguments and make it so difficult to counter them. The real difficulty, the main stumbling block, is the way traditional religions associate God exclusively with their opinions. You can argue against an obvious human injustice, you can demonstrate the absurdity of a particular type of intolerance, you can poke fun at bigotry and hatred, but how can you argue against God? This is the real difficulty religions face in every area of human development. If they weld particular phases of human life and cultural development to the will and commandment of their God, how can they ever make changes to their life? That is why many people believe that traditional religions are incapable of making these liberating changes, so they abandon them as primitive superstitions incapable of development. It was why many feminists abandoned Christianity while it was debating rather than celebrating the equality of women with men. They saw it as incurably patriarchal and oppressive towards women, in both its theology and its structures. What frustrated feminists most in their debate with Christianity was not that the men in charge said they did not want to share power with women, nor that men liked all the male language about God in the Bible because it flattered their own sense of gender superiority – there would have been a certain kind of honesty in that, and the laughter it provoked might itself have been cleansing and transforming. But that's not what they said. They said, 'We ourselves have no prejudices against women; indeed, if it were up to us, we would alter things to accommodate their obvious frustrations; unfortunately, God has different ideas. He has fixed these things for ever, and who are we to fight against God?'

A preposterous claim like that brings us to the real point of decision, and our response to it will determine whether the Church can be allowed to find a way of responding to the best of contemporary aspirations, or whether it is destined for ever to be locked into a world view that is simply incredible to thoughtful people in our time. If we deny the very best of modern aspirations, the longing for justice, freedom and tolerance, and bind God inextricably to attitudes that run counter to this energy of liberation, then we are simply identifying God with a previous social dispensation, and God becomes a fetish, a way of supporting our own discomfort with the tide of history. If we put the so-called mind of God in opposition, not to the selfishness and spiritual poverty of contemporary society, but to its genuine moral discoveries and its desire, however incomplete, to affirm and accept men and women in their wonderful variety, then society will be justified in its rejection of us, because to do otherwise would be to turn its back upon its own best discoveries. This is always the great tension in traditional religions, but we can learn to deal with it by recognising the symbolic and revisable nature of all human claims about God and the dynamic, surprise-laden nature of the God we struggle to talk about.

The Old Testament scholar Walter Brueggemann said that it is the Torah that overturns the Torah, it is God who revises God, God who calls us away from where we think God has been to where God wants us to be, only to be called again to move on, movement and change being the dominant characteristics of the moral life. Whether this is because God is an entirely human construct on to which we project our highest values and our struggle to achieve them; or because God is real and patiently prods us into the goodness we are so resistant to; the issue is the same: the endless human struggle to live just and virtuous lives, an ambition that is riddled with paradoxes. A reading of history shows us that our understanding of morality has been fluid and dynamic from the beginning, which is why Nietzsche (as we have previously seen) told us that:

ARE CHRISTIANS ALLOWED TO BE GAY?

. . . everything good was once new, consequently unfamiliar, contrary to custom, *immoral,* and gnawed at the heart of its fortunate inventor like a worm.[2]

And we have already noted how Isaiah Berlin pointed out that the difficulty of the moral life is that it is rarely a conflict between an obvious good and an obvious evil, but usually between rival versions of the good. That is why loyalty or faithfulness to a religious or moral tradition can lead us into injustice, so an examination of the place of loyalty in religious and moral traditions is a good place to begin an examination of the moral life. The fact is, we are all born embedded in a moral tradition, whether mediated by religion or society, and moral stability emphasises the importance of loyalty in that context – it is what keeps things steady. The paradox is that if we are more loyal to the institutions that mediate our morality than to the principles of morality itself, our loyalty becomes a form of unacknowledged injustice.

In our day we are learning to read the Bible in a different way; not as a fixed and unchanging law, but as the flawed and fallible record of where previous generations got to in understanding the nature of their relationship with God. That is why the Bible, though it is one of our greatest treasures, is also our greatest danger. We are always tempted to misuse it, by turning it into an oracle to interpret our present time, rather than acknowledging it as a witness to the way our forebears responded to what was present to them. This is why we get into those unedifying arguments about the application of particular texts to our own dilemmas. There is, for example, the interminable dispute over the precise interpretation of the few texts in the Bible that mention same-sex relations, as though we were made for the text, and not the text for us. We have recently abandoned the text's tyranny over women, as we abandoned its justification of slavery, and soon we'll abandon its ignorant misunderstanding of homosexuality. The real issue ought to be not the meaning of the texts themselves, but the appalling way they have been used as a justification for the persecution and punishment of those who are different. Amnesty International's 1995 report, *Breaking the Silence*, was a horrifying catalogue of human rights violations against people based on their sexual orientation. The report contained dozens of carefully documented cases from countries all over the world. It shows us that, three quarters of a century after Hitler's extermination policy for gays and other so-called social deviants blackened the skies of Europe with smoke from the gas ovens, homophobia is still alive and violently kicking, and much of it is motivated by religious zeal.

And it has to be acknowledged that there is a dynamic connection between the theological rejection of gay and lesbian people, based on the ancient texts in question, and the persecution and abuse they have endured over the centuries; just as there is an obvious connection between anti-Semitic rhetoric in the New Testament and the centuries of persecution that climaxed in the horrors of the Holocaust in Hitler's gas ovens. There is a staggering moral disproportion between the neurotic preoccupation with the precise interpretation of an obscure, ancient text, and indifference to the suffering it brings on actual, living people who become the text's victims. That's why I want to get back to Wilfred Owen and what he can represent for us.

Owen's relationship with the social and political establishment was instructive. He despised how it put its own survival before the lives of its individual members. Established systems always do this. There is even a philosophical argument of some merit that justifies it. It is argued that it is expedient to let this group or that group suffer, rather than let the whole people perish. It is better to turn a blind eye to an obvious injustice, if removing it will threaten the stability of the system itself. This is a political rather than a moral logic, but it has been used by leaders throughout history to justify injustice when powerful interests are opposed to its removal. One even has to have a certain compassion for the leaders caught up in these moral dilemmas: faced with the suffering of particular groups, their desire to offer comfort and relief is weakened, and sometimes finally conquered, by the knowledge that to do so will enrage the groups for whom the injustice in question is a matter of fundamental belief.

Every minority in history has been caught in this bind: racial minorities are the classic example, but so are women; and it is where lesbian and gay people find themselves today. It is not much comfort to be told that history is on your side and that the changes will come in the churches that have already come in society. This is where Wilfred Owen's example helps. He performed an act of internal emigration that enabled him to live physically within the structure he despised, while living spiritually in the country of his own integrity. He made a journey towards himself that enabled him to ignore all the voices that denied his authenticity, and in making that journey he found his voice. And he used that voice as an advocate for the doomed youth of his generation. He identified with the victims of the system he despised, the system of which he was a subversive official, an enemy within, and gave voice to their suffering.

Spiritual cleansing and moral challenge always come to self-satisfied institutions from the edges, rarely from the centre. You are on one of society's edges, so you could become the poets of the outcast, the singers of the despised – and not just of gay and lesbian people. In E.M. Forster's great imperative, 'Only connect': connect your own experience to that of sufferers everywhere, and find solidarity with them. The gay and lesbian vocation is a call to stand with those who are the victims of power's arrogance, wherever it is found. It is a call not only to the struggle, but to the spirituality of identification, and the moral imperative that makes connections. The human struggle contains, but is about more than gay and lesbian liberation. As I salute you in your struggle, and through you thank the many gay people who have ministered grace and love to me, I want to remind you of the joy that Wilfred Owen found in the truth that took him to so early a death, a death he anticipated. The struggle towards a larger humanity is itself a kind of war, but in war there are meetings with strangers, even enemies, who become allies and friends. In one of his most powerful poems, Owen imagined just such a meeting in a dream that sounds like a premonition of his own death. I'll end with it:

ARE CHRISTIANS ALLOWED TO BE GAY?

It seemed that out of battle I escaped
Down some profound dull tunnel, long since scooped
Through granites which titanic wars had groined.
Yet also there encumbered sleepers groaned,
Too fast in thought or death to be bestirred.
Then, as I probed them, one sprang up, and stared
With piteous recognition in fixed eyes,
Lifting distressful hands as if to bless.
And by his smile, I knew that sullen hall,
By his dead smile, I knew we stood in Hell.
With a thousand pains that vision's face was grained;
Yet no blood reached there from the upper ground,
And no guns thumped, or down the flues made moan.
'Strange friend,' I said, 'here is no cause to mourn.'
'None,' said the other, 'save the undone years,
The hopelessness. Whatever hope is yours,
Was my life also; I went hunting wild
After the wildest beauty in the world,
Which lies not calm in eyes, or braided hair,
But mocks the steady running of the hour,
And if it grieves, grieves richlier than here.
For of my glee might many men have laughed,
And of my weeping something had been left,
Which must die now. I mean the truth untold,
The pity of war, the pity war distilled.
Now men will go content with what we spoiled,
Or, discontent, boil bloody, and be spilled.
They will be swift with swiftness of the tigress.

ON REFLECTION

None will break ranks, though nations trek from
    progress.
Courage was mine, and I had mystery;
Wisdom was mine, and I had mastery:
To miss the march of this retreating world
Into vain citadels that are not walled.
Then, when much blood had clogged their
    chariot-wheels,
I would go up and wash them from sweet wells,
Even with truths that lie too deep for taint.
I would have poured my spirit without stint
But not through wounds; not on the cess of war.
Foreheads of men have bled where no wounds were.
I am the enemy you killed, my friend.
I knew you in this dark: for so you frowned
Yesterday through me as you jabbed and killed.
I parried; but my hands were loath and cold.
Let us sleep now . . .'[3]

21

THIS IS IT

Very few people remember Alan Watts today, but he was a significant figure in the counterculture of the 1960s. It was a turbulent and liberating decade that, in the words of the French poet Charles Péguy, began in politics and ended in mysticism, which exactly described my own experience. I began the Sixties leading rent strikes and banning the bomb in Glasgow; I ended it standing on my head at a yoga centre in Edinburgh. Now, it is impossible for a Scotsman to stand on his head unself-consciously, which brings me back to Alan Watts. By the end of the Sixties our failure to change the world through politics led many people on the mystical quest, so the great journey to the East began, and Alan Watts was one of the guides. Watts had been an Anglican priest, but he gave it up, moved to California and became one of the gurus of the so-called counterculture and an expert on Eastern philosophy.

Like a Scotsman standing on his head, it is very difficult to make that sort of migration without watching yourself doing it, and there was something self-conscious about Alan Watts, something self-referential, something that did not quite ring true, though there was truth in it.

Monica Furlong wrote an affectionate biography of him, entitled, *Genuine Fake: A Biography of Alan Watts,* and the title captured the enigmatic quality of the man. In Saint Paul's language, he was a true imposter. He was flawed, spiritually and morally, but he was never a cynic and he was far from indifferent to the sacred matters he traded in. He knew his own poverty, yet he did genuinely enrich others spiritually and open new paths for them. He enjoyed the adulation he received, liked being a guru, especially to attractive women, but he was serious about life and made some genuine discoveries that he generously shared.

Watts's most important message was expressed through the ambiguity of his own life. Yet I realise as I utter that word 'ambiguity' that I have myself fallen into the trap he wanted people to avoid. The theological description of this trap is dualism, the idea that the sphere of the holy and the sphere of the human are somehow separate, so that to be holy or to be a vehicle of holiness for others, you have to deny the messy actuality of your own life and try to become something you are not. There is nothing ambiguous about the fact that we, in all our confusion and brokenness, can still mediate God to one another. Watts wrote:

> The spiritual is not to be separated from the material, nor the wonderful from the ordinary. We need, above all, to disentangle ourselves from habits of speech and thought which make it impossible for us to see that this – the immediate, everyday, and present experience – is IT, the entire and ultimate point for the existence of a universe.

This is IT, this is where it happens, this is where we meet the other; not somewhere else, as someone else, someone better, someone different, someone made perfect. No, it is here in our genuine fraudulence, our spiritual sensuality, our affluent poverty, our joyful sorrowing, our fractured wholeness that we experience ultimate reality – which Watts called IT – and say 'Yes' to it. All false dualisms are ended. There is no separation between the mystical and the political, not even in a motivational sense. It is not that I pray and, as a result of my prayer, am led to campaign against racism or homophobia. It is not that I commit myself to a spiritual discipline and, as a result of my effort, am led to struggle for the transformation of society. The trouble with bad religion is that it slices experience up into departments like that and actually takes us out of life. One test of that is to examine how you feel after some church services, or encounters with some kinds of religious people, compared to your feelings after a great concert or a terrific movie or an amusing and stimulating meal with friends. The former squeezes life out of you, diminishes you; while the other experiences enlarge you, make you more generous, more human, more in touch with others, part of them, glad to be human, moved by the kindness of strangers, lifted up by the transcendence of another's vision of things, another's take on this unrepeatably marvellous experience called life. Bad religion takes us out of life, makes us suspicious of it, anxious about it, afraid to get it wrong, because it sets God and God's creation in opposition. And we end up sacrificing the enjoyment of life for control over life. We create domination systems, religious and political, that substitute power for pleasure, dictation over people, rather than celebration of them. Pleasure haters become persecutors very easily. They hated Jesus as much for his obvious pleasure in eating and drinking with his disreputable friends as for his challenge to the political and religious domination systems that oppressed them. The best revolutions are prompted not by the politics of envy, but by the politics of joy, the passionate ambition to include everyone in the feast of life. The best socialists are the champagne socialists, the ones who enjoy life and want everyone else to enjoy it more abundantly. On Judgement Day, God is going to challenge us about why we did not more enjoy the life we had been given and share the joy of it with others.

We are going to have to rediscover the theology of the happy remnant in our day, the theology of those who bear witness to the joy of God in a time of condemnation, the possibility of the grace of God in a time of punishing certainties. Our vocation today is to continue to be people to whom and through whom that can happen. It is our calling to deny the false polarities of fundamentalism and secularism, and go on defiantly expressing the unities of flesh and spirit, mind and mystery, tradition and reason, scripture and experience, not deny them by allowing ourselves to be lured into the seductive dualisms that separate God and nature. There is no separation, except in our own heads, our own divided consciousness. If we commit ourselves to that fateful split, either of two things can happen, particularly to the clergy, the officers of divided consciousness. Either you come to believe it, believe you have to become spiritual and holy, a sort of ambulatory stained-glass window, so you begin to look and talk like one, and end up like those caricatures comedians love to take off on television. Or you become paralysed by your own unlikeness to the perfect model, your own failure to be perfect, and you become a divided self, a liar who has to speak the truth, an empty person who has to go on giving when there is nothing left to give, a doubter who has to preach the faith. The reconciliation comes when you recognise that THIS IS IT; that it is from the actual human situation and no other that you minister, from within your doubts and weaknesses, so the only real failure is to lie to yourself about who and what you are.

There is a human experience that sometimes captures the mystery of the other that haunts us, becomes co-equal with it, almost becomes it. Music is normally held to be the experience that does this best. It is what George Steiner called 'the perfect tautology of form and content'. It evidences itself, is itself the experience we experience and not just a sign or symbol for something else. Art, music, poetry, are all priestly in their ministry, because they unite us with transcendence and place us in its midst, rather than talk about it, talk unceasingly and ineffectively about it, which is what the Church usually does. Recently I've been reading the poems of Norman MacCaig as part of my daily spiritual exercises. A MacCaig poem does more than talk about something, it is that something, it is one of Steiner's perfect tautologies, it actually puts you in the midst of the thing celebrated. Here is 'July Evening':

> A bird's voice chinks and tinkles
> Alone in the gaunt reedbed –
> Tiny silversmith
> Working late in the evening.

ON REFLECTION

I sit and listen. The rooftop
With a quill of smoke stuck in it
Wavers against the sky
In the dreamy heat of summer.

Flowers' closing time: bee lurches
Across the hayfield, singing
And feeling its drunken way
Round the air's invisible corners.

And grass is grace. And charlock
Is gold of its own bounty.
The broken chair by the wall
Is one with immortal landscapes.

Something has been completed
That everything is part of,
Something that will go on
Being completed forever.[1]

Unless we can, at least some of the time, dispose ourselves to be instruments of a similar, a divine tautology, we are largely wasting our time. People don't want to hear us talking about God, as though we knew what we were talking about; but they will pay attention if they can join us in experiencing God. Increasingly, it seems to me, the Church should stop just talking about God and start being the place where God may be experienced. We should be God's poets and musicians. In poets and musicians, the gift of attention is acute: they look and listen with such self-emptying intensity that they almost become what they look at and listen to, so that it is made present through their art, is made flesh. Like all truth, Christian living is a paradox in which we are encouraged to be utterly ourselves, because it is the undivided self that is the instrument of that depth in life we call holiness; but we are also called to pay attention, to look and listen, and not allow ourselves to get in the way of the mystery that wants to express itself through us. You don't resolve paradoxes; you live them.

The paradox that some of us are going to have to start living is that it is religion itself that can be the greatest threat to God and the life God gives us. This is because of the ancient human fear of living without a script, of having to find our own lines, make our own responses to the beautiful and tragic immediacy of life. God is the great jazz musician who wants us to get the feel of things and improvise freely, using but not being bound by the melodies that are around, the tunes handed down to us in the tradition. God wants us to listen to one another, to pay attention to the other's pain and joy and weave it into our music, make it a dynamic, living tradition, so that we can move with the fluidity of it all. But religion has taught us to fear this kind of creative recklessness, because it believes that life is a music test rather than a rolling jazz session, and God is an official examiner rather than the great trumpeter of creation. That's where all the fear comes from.

Jesus tried to blow away that fear by warning us about the danger of religion. That is what the parable of the Good Samaritan is about. It is not a parable about religious hypocrisy, about professing one thing and doing another.

ON REFLECTION

The point of the parable is that the Priest and the Levite were obedient adherents of a strict religious code. When they saw the man lying by the roadside, they asked themselves if the script of their religion permitted them to do anything, allowed them to be neighbour to the one who had fallen among thieves. And the answer they reached was the correct one, because it was written that they could not be a neighbour to a sinner or a gentile. The code was clear, the text was exact, as texts frequently are. The Samaritan followed the same code, heretic though he was. The text also bound him and gave him the same answer. But something happened to him. At the heart of the parable there is a single, convulsive verb, *esplanknisthe*, translated into Scots by William Lorimer as, 'his heart was sair for him'. He was consumed with pity for the man by the roadside, and it was that dynamic pity that overcame the code that bound him and gave him the courage to tear up the script that dictated his life. Compassion overcame code, life in all its complexity asserted itself against the tidy script of religion.

It is a dangerous way to live, of course, because it will put us on a collision course with those who think they are in charge, the concert-hall managers, the chorus writers, the guardians of the text, those who own the copyright on the official and only playable anthem. But look out, look ahead, get out of the hall, out from behind the closed doors, the real festival is happening elsewhere and God is calling us to join it.

22

LISTENING

I wrote my first book fifty years ago, and I read it again recently. I was impressed by the passion of the young man who wrote it, but depressed by his assertive, hectoring tone. It reminded me of something Bertrand Russell said: 'Zeal is a bad mark for a cause; no one is zealous for the two-times table; we're only zealous about things we can't be quite sure about and it makes us anxious.' Reading what I wrote fifty years ago, I can hear that young man trying to silence or suppress his own doubts.

But what was he shouting about? The biggest question we humans ask ourselves: is God real? And we can't help asking that question. It comes with our humanity, this strange nature we have that is obsessed with its own existence. Does life mean anything? Is there some reality behind it that *meant* it, gave it purpose? Those were the questions that obsessed the young man fifty years ago, and still obsesses the old man today. But my perspective has shifted, so that I am now more interested in *how* we argue this and other great questions than in the answers we give. That's because I have changed my mind on this great question many times – yet remain the same person. I have had to learn to live with myself and my disagreements with myself over a lifetime of inner argument. So: what I have learned during this lifetime of arguing with myself? Above all, the need for modesty and humility in the claims we make about how we see things; but without letting it paralyse us into passivity and inactivity.

Let me try to explain, using a parable taught by the spiritual leaders of Jainism, an ancient Indian religion that believed we should always try to avoid violence in our lives, even in how we think. They told a story about six blind men who were invited by their teacher to describe an elephant by feeling different parts of its body. The man who felt the tail said the elephant was like a rope. The man who felt the leg said it was like a pillar. And so on. Their teacher told them that while each of them was correct in their description of the part of the elephant they had touched, none had grasped the reality of the whole elephant. The moral was that humans, by definition, were limited in their grasp of reality. We see things not as *they are*, but as *we are*. And we might even see things from different angles as we travel through life; our view changing, as mine has, frequently. It all goes to show what a shifting kaleidoscope the human mind is. I have learned two things from thinking about all this.

The first idea to register is that human conflict and disagreement are not abnormal interludes in our history; they are its permanent state, its enduring condition. Crisis is our normality; it comes with these big, conflicted minds of ours that constantly struggle with the questions life brings. But uncertainty is such an uncomfortable state to be in that we constantly search for ways out of it, and in history two big escape routes always seem to suggest themselves.

One is the idea that out there somewhere there is a Great Leader, who will lead us out of all our confusions into the Promised Land of absolute certainty and permanent stability. Fifty years ago, I was trying to persuade myself that I knew exactly what God's plan for humanity was; today the longing for the Great Deliverer is more focused on politics than it is on religion. But it's the same kind of magical thinking. And it's why our history is littered with examples of great leaders we rushed to follow, certain they would lead us to peace and paradise – and all they did was lead us to hell.

The other escape route is the idea that somewhere there is a blueprint or plan for a perfect society that will rescue us from all these conflicts, if only we can find the recipe and impose or apply it. The recipes have varied in history, lunging from the far left to the far right, but none of them has ever delivered the Promised Land in all the perfection we long for.

There is something religious about both these deep longings, even in their secular forms, that is why they are so difficult to shake off. They appear and reappear constantly in human history. And they are not absent today.

But the other thing I've learned is that we must not let our scepticism about these great delusions paralyse us into despair and inactivity. We may never be able to achieve the permanently perfect society, but we can work to make things better in the muddled society we live in. Knowing how flawed we are and how fearful we are of our own excesses – of opinion as well as action – we should practise our disagreements with a lightness of touch that may help us change direction when we need to. This is the way

ON REFLECTION

slow revolutions are accomplished. The biggest revolution of my lifetime has been in the status of women, *because we learned to change our minds and listen to others!*

As I've learned from my own experience, true believers, either in religion or politics, don't listen – they shout, because they're not as sure about things as they appear to be. And ours is a very shouty time, isn't it? All those angry voices and livid faces screaming at each other. Let's turn the volume down. Let's listen more and shout less. You'd be surprised what you might learn. You might even change your mind.

It was an Israeli poet, Yehuda Amichai, who really taught me this in one simple and profound poem. Here it is:

> From the place where we are right
> Flowers will never grow
> In the Spring.
>
> The place where we are right
> Is hard and trampled
> Like a yard.
>
> But doubts and loves
> Dig up the world
> Like a mole, a plough.
> And a whisper will be heard in the place
> Where the ruined
> House once stood.[1]

Let us stop shouting and start listening.

23

KEEPING ON KEEPING CHRISTMAS

Christmas Eve services are the busiest in the year for the Christian Church. Most of the people who crowd in at midnight are practising, believing Christians, but a significant minority are not. They are best described as wistful non-believers, and some of the best twentieth-century poems about Christmas are written from their point of view. They come from writers who once belonged to the community of faith but are no longer able to believe, so they look back on the magic of Christmas with an affectionate, almost sorrowing unbelief. But their mood is not one of confident disbelief; it is less certain than that; it has a wistful note to it, expressing a regret that belief is no longer possible but wishing, almost, that it were. One of the best of these poems of regret is 'The Oxen' by Thomas Hardy, which refers to the old Christian belief that in the stable at Bethlehem where Jesus was born and laid in a manger, even the animals knelt in worship before him:

ON REFLECTION

Christmas Eve, and twelve of the clock.
    'Now they are all on their knees,'
An elder said as we sat in a flock
    By the embers in hearthside ease.

We pictured the meek mild creatures where
    They dwelt in their strawy pen,
Nor did it occur to one of us there
    To doubt they were kneeling then.

So far a fancy few would weave
    In these years! Yet, I feel,
If someone said on Christmas Eve,
    'Come; see the oxen kneel

'In the lonely barton by yonder coomb
    Our childhood used to know,'
I should go with him in the gloom,
    Hoping it might be so.'[1]

That kind of wistful looking back, 'hoping it might be so', is a mood that poets capture to perfection. And that is exactly what Cecil Day Lewis tried to do in a poem he wrote about remembering the Christmases he loved as a child. In the poem, the people he describes as 'children of unbelief' are old and approaching the end of their lives. The poet invites them to come outside and look in through the window of memory at themselves when they were young and eagerly excited by what Christmas might bring them.

KEEPING ON KEEPING CHRISTMAS

Come out for a while and look from the outside in
At a room you know
As the firelight fitfully beats on the windowpane –
An old heart sinking low,
And the whispering melting kisses of the snow
Soothe time from your brow.

It is Christmastide. Does the festival promise as fairly
As ever to you? I feel
The numbers of one whose drifted years conceal
His original landmarks of good and ill.
For a heart weighed down by its own and the world's
   folly
This season has little appeal.

But tomorrow is Christmas Day. Can it really mean
Nothing to you? It is hard
To see it as more than a time-worn, tinsel routine,
Or else a night incredibly starred,
Angels, oxen, a Babe – the recurrent dream
Of a Christmas card.

You must try again. Say 'Christmas Eve'. Now,
   quick,
What do you see?
'I see in the firelit room a child awake,
Mute with expectancy
For the berried day, the presents, the Christmas cake.
Is he mine? or me?'

> He is you and yours. Desiring for him tomorrow's
> Feast – the crackers, the Tree, the piled
> Presents – you lose yourself in his yearning, and
>   borrow
> His eyes to behold
> Your own young world again. Love's mystery is
>   revealed
> When the father becomes the child.
> 'Yet would it make those carolling angels weep
> To think how Incarnate Love
> Means such trivial joys to us children of unbelief?'
> No. It's a miracle great enough
> If through centuries, clouded and dingy, this Day can
>   keep
> Expectation alive.²

That's a very modern voice, expressing the complicated attitude of today's 'children of unbelief', who – if only for one day a year – would love to recover the magic of Christmas, but find it impossible to keep their scepticism at bay. The English poet John Betjeman understood the difficulty well.

Betjeman was a Christian believer, but he had doubts, and they were with him till the end of his life. But he knew that faith and doubt always went together, descanting on each other like two singers, because the opposite of faith was never doubt, it was certainty. We don't doubt the two-times-table because we don't have to 'believe' it. We *know* it's true; we can even do it on our fingers. But we can't know for certain that God exists, and that the universe, in spite of all its sorrow and suffering, has an ultimate purpose and meaning. We hope it might be so. We trust or believe it might be so, but we have our doubts. And our doubts have their own sad beauty. Betjeman's doubts produced some of his best poetry, and you catch the tone in his famous poem about Christmas:

> The bells of waiting Advent ring,
> The Tortoise stove is lit again
> And lamp-oil light across the night
> Has caught the streaks of winter rain
> In many a stained-glass window sheen
> From Crimson Lake to Hooker's Green.
>
> The holly in the windy hedge
> And round the Manor House the yew
> Will soon be stripped to deck the ledge,
> The altar, font and arch and pew,
> So that the villagers can say
> 'The church looks nice' on Christmas day.
>
> Provincial public houses blaze
> And Corporation tramcars clang,
> On lighted tenements I gaze
> Where paper decorations hang,
> And bunting in the red Town Hall
> Says 'Merry Christmas to you all'.

> And London shops on Christmas Eve
> Are strung with silver bells and flowers
> As hurrying clerks the City leave
> To pigeon-haunted classic towers,
> And marbled clouds go scudding by
> The many-steepled London sky.
>
> And girls in slacks remember Dad,
> And oafish louts remember Mum,
> And sleepless children's hearts are glad,
> And Christmas-morning bells say 'Come!'
> Even to shining ones who dwell
> Safe in the Dorchester hotel.
>
> And is it true? And is it true,
> This most tremendous tale of all
> Seen in a stained-glass window's hue.
>   A Baby in an ox's stall?
> The Maker of the stars and sea
> Become a Child on earth for me?[3]

Fortunately, you don't have to be a convinced Christian believer to enjoy Christmas. The other reason for celebrating it is that it cheers us up in the darkest days of winter. And that's why the Church chose what Christina Rossetti's famous carol calls 'the bleak midwinter' as the best time of year to celebrate the birth of Jesus. We don't know exactly when Jesus was born, either the day or the year, but when the Western Church decided to celebrate his birth on 25 December, they were Christening an old pagan festival that marked the day of the winter solstice, the day the sun began its slow journey north after the darkest day of winter. That's why we can all celebrate Christmas, whether or not we believe, in Betjeman's words, that it was the day on which 'the Maker of the stars and sea [has] become a Child on earth for me'. We can celebrate it because it cheers us all up in the middle of winter, just when we need it most. So, whether you are a believer or a non-believer, Christmas is always worth celebrating. And I'll give Glasgow's own poet, Edwin Morgan, the last word.

> Coming up Buchanan Street, quickly, on a sharp
>   winter evening
> a young man and two girls, under the Christmas
>   lights –
> The young man carries a new guitar in his arms,
> the girl on the inside carries a very young baby,
> and the girl on the outside carries a chihuahua.
> And the three of them are laughing, their breath rises
> in a cloud of happiness, and as they pass
> the boy says, 'Wait till he sees this but!'
> The chihuahua has a tiny Royal Stewart tartan coat
>   like a teapot-holder,
> the baby in its white shawl is all bright eyes and
>   mouth like favours in a fresh sweet cake,
> the guitar swells out under its milky plastic cover, tied
>   at the neck with silver tinsel tape and a brisk sprig
>   of mistletoe.
> Orphean sprig! Melting baby! Warm chihuahua!
> The vale of tears is powerless before you.
> Whether Christ is born, or is not born, you
> put paid to fate, it abdicates

ON REFLECTION

under the Christmas lights.
Monsters of the year
go blank, are scattered back,
can't bear this march of three.

— And the three have passed, vanished in the crowd
(yet not vanished, for in their arms they wind
the life of men and beasts, and music,
laughter ringing them round like a guard)
at the end of this winter's day.[4]

24

THANKING

Some of us, perhaps foolishly, are haunted by the question: what does the *universe* mean? A possible answer may lie in the fact that we can and do find meaning in music and pictures without words, without explanation. So maybe that's the approach we should try here. Let me explain what I am trying to say.

Two very confident answers have been given to the question, what does the universe *mean*? Notice first that it's a sneaky question, because in its most usual form it hides a qualifying term, the word *ultimately*. What we are really asking is whether the universe has a *final* or *ultimate purpose*? Whether there is some transcendent intelligence outside it that *meant* it? Most of us find lots of non-ultimate meanings for our lives in the universe in which we find ourselves. Wealth, fame, happiness, love, art are just a few of them. But what can we do with the question of *ultimate* meaning? I want to look at two answers, neither of which satisfies me, and then suggest a third.

Both unsatisfactory answers are big and confident, which is maybe why I am uneasy with them. One is that the ultimate meaning or purpose of the universe lies in the will of a transcendent being we call 'God', and that our purpose is to find out and obey what God demands of us; the difficulty being that there are many conflicting versions of what the divine will for us might be – hence the unending disputes theology has with itself.

The other big, confident answer is that the universe has no ultimate meaning, no purpose. It is just a big machine that manufactured itself out of nowhere billions of years ago and will disappear again billions of years hence. And it is as indifferent to us as the vehicle that took us to work this morning.

Here's my problem with both these big, confident answers. There is a pass I walk between two high hills that makes me want to cry out with gratitude for its beauty – but who is there to thank? I know it is unlikely that there was ever a divine artist who crafted these hills like a sculptor moulding clay. I know they were formed millions of years ago by insensate continents of ice crashing against each other, yet today they make me cry out with joy. But if God didn't make them, who is there to thank? Can I thank Nothing? For years I didn't think so, till a poet taught me how to do it, and a poet of sorrow, a poet crushed by a death machine that was as indifferent to human love as those rolling continents of ice. His name was Paul Celan. Born in 1920 into a Jewish family in what is now Romania, his parents died in the death camps of the Nazi Holocaust. Yet out of that horror, that grinding machine of slaughter, Celan wrote some of the most beautiful and searching poetry of the twentieth century. Here, again, is his Psalm of praise to Nothing, 'De Nichts':

THANKING

No one moulds us again out of earth and clay,
No one conjures our dust.
No one.
Praised be your name, no one . . .
A nothing
We were, are, shall
Remain, flowering . . .

What am I saying here? Something simple. Thinking will never resolve the big debate about meaning, which is why our answers go on grinding against each other like the ice that sculpted my beloved hills. So, why not, at least some of the time, stop thinking and start thanking, even if it is Nothing – Celan's poem 'De Nichts' – we find ourselves having to thank? That, anyway, is where I find myself in my latter days, as old age creeps over me. And it is poets who've been my best teachers. W.H. Auden advised me to let my last thinks all be thanks, and that is what I have tried to do here.

NOTES

Chapter 1
1 James Charlton, 'Simone Weil at Saint-Marcel d'Ardèche', in *So Much Light*, Pardalote Press: Tasmania, 2007, p.26.

Chapter 3
1 W.B. Yeats, 'The Circus Animals' Desertion', *The Poems*, Ed. Daniel Albright, Everyman: London, 1994, p.394.
2 Ibid. p.844.
3 Ibid. p.394.
4 Ibid. p.844.
5 Lewis Hyde, *The Gift: How the Creative Spirit Transforms the World*, Canongate: Edinburgh 2006, p.193.
6 Gospel of Mark, 15:31.
7 Tennessee Williams, *Cat on a Hot Tin Roof and Other Plays*, Penguin Books: London, 1976, p.7.
8 Ibid. pp.317–8.
9 Ibid. p.308.
10 Ibid. p.304.
11 Edwin Muir, 'Scotland 1941', *Selected Poems*, Faber and Faber: London, 1965, p.34.
12 George Mackay Brown, 'The Storm', *The Collected Poems of George Mackay Brown*, John Murray: London, 2006, p.3.
13 Iain Crichton Smith, 'Old Woman', *Selected Poems*, Carcanet Press: Manchester, 1985, p.18.
14 Iain Crichton Smith, 'She Teaches Lear', *Selected Poems*, Carcanet Press: Manchester, 1985, p.54.

15 T.C. Smout, *A History of the Scottish People*, Fontana Press: London, 1998, p.93.
16 Cyril Connolly, *The Unquiet Grave*, Curwen Press: London, 1944, under the pseudonym 'Palinurus'.
17 George Steiner, *Heidegger*, Fontana: London, 1992, p.136.
18 In Iris Murdoch, *The Sovereignty of Good*, Arc: London, 1985, p.59.
19 Iain Crichton Smith, 'She Teaches Lear', *Selected Poems*, Carcanet Press: Manchester, 1985, p.52.
20 Ibid; 'Old Woman', *Selected Poems*, Carcanet Press: Manchester, 1985, p.18.

Chapter 4
1 W.H. Auden, 'Twelve Songs IX', *Collected Poems*, Faber and Faber: London 1976, p.120.
2 W.H. Auden, *Forewords and Afterwards*, Faber and Faber: London, 1973.
3 Dietrich Bonhoeffer, *Letters and Papers from Prison*, SCM: London, 1971, p.369.
4 Auden, p.509.
5 Auden, p.215.
6 Alan Bennett, *Keeping On Keeping On*, Faber and Faber: London, 2016, p.325.

Chapter 5
1 William Shakespeare, *Twelfth Night*, Act 2, Scene 3.
2 John Calvin, *Institutes of the Christian Religion*, Book 3, Chapter 21.
3 James Joyce, *Portrait of the Artist as a Young Man*, Penguin Books: London, 1916, p.121.
4 Robert Burns, 'Holy Willie's Prayer', *Selected Poems*, Penguin Books: London, 1993, p.30
5 James Hogg, *Confessions of a Justified Sinner*, Canongate: Edinburgh, 1991, p.100.
6 Ibid. p.162.
7 Ibid. p.164.
8 Ibid. p.166.
9 Ibid. p.166.
10 William Shakespeare, *Twelfth Night*, Act 5, Scene 1.

NOTES

Chapter 6
1 Martin Heidegger, *Being and Time*, Fontana: London, 1992, p.136.
2 Dora Carrington, '16 February 1932', in *Letters and Extracts from Her Diaries*. Jonathan Cape: London, 1970.
3 'Hymn 351', *Hymnal for Scotland*, Oxford University Press: Oxford, 1956.
4 Bernard O'Donoghue, 'Going Without Saying', in *Being Alive*, Ed. Neil Astley, Bloodaxe Books: Hexham, 2004, p.448.

Chapter 7
1 John Hick, *The Fifth Dimension*, One Word: Oxford, 1999, p.42.
2 Friedrich Nietzsche, *A Nietzsche Reader*, Penguin Classics: London, 1977, p.82.

Chapter 8
1 Bruce Chatwin, *What Am I Doing Here*, Picador: London, 1988.
2 Gerard Manley Hopkins, 'God's Grandeur', *Collected Poems*, Oxford University Press: Oxford, 1948, p.70.
3 J.A. Baker, 'The Peregrine', *New York Review of Books*, 1967, p.14.
4 Ibid.

Chapter 9
1 Graham Greene, *The Human Factor*, Bodley Head: Oxford, 1978, pp.333–4.
2 Friedrich Nietzsche, *Human, All-Too-Human*, Section: 224, translated by Helen Zimmern, T.N. Foulis: Edinburgh and London, 1909. Accessed via Project Gutenberg.
3 John Henry Newman, *Apologia Pro Vita Sua*, 1864, originally issued in weekly parts, reissued in Everyman's Library, 1912.
4 Simone Weil, *The Iliad, or the Poem of Force*, Grove Press: New York, 1986, p.163.
5 Simone Weil, *Essay on Force*, ibid.
6 Fyodor Dostoevsky, *The Brothers Karamazov*, Everyman's Library: New York, 1997, p.262.

Chapter 10
1 Friedrich Nietzsche, *Human, All-Too-Human*, Section 5, translated

by Helen Zimmern, T.N. Foulis: Edinburgh and London, 1909. Accessed via Project Gutenberg.
2 Bishop Butler to John Wesley.
3 Callum G. Brown, *The Death of Christian Britain*, Routledge: London, 2000.
4 The Letter to James, 1:17: 'Every good and perfect gift is from above, and cometh down from the Father of lights, with whom is no variableness, neither shadow of turning.'
5 Voltaire, *Philosophical Dictionary*, in *An Enlightenment Reader*, Penguin Books: London, 1995, p.131.
6 Ibid. p.130.
7 Malise Ruthven, *Fundamentalism*, Oxford University Press: Oxford, 2004.
8 George Santayana, *Life of Reason: Flux and Continuity in Human Nature*, Vol.1. Chapter XII, originally published in five volumes 1905–6, reissued by MIT Press, 2011.

Chapter 11
1 Gerard Manley Hopkins, 'Spring and Fall: To a Young Child', *Poems*, Oxford University Press: London, 1948, p.94.
2 Friedrich Nietzsche, *Human, All-Too-Human*, Section 224, translated by Helen Zimmern, T.N. Foulis: Edinburgh and London, 1909. Accessed via Project Gutenberg.
3 Ibid.
4 Michel Foucault, *The Use of Pleasure*, Penguin Books: London, 1992, p.116.
5 Richard Dawkins, *The Devil's Chaplain*, Weidenfeld and Nicolson: London, 2003, p.12.

Chapter 12
1 James Joyce, *Portrait of the Artist as a Young Man*, Penguin: London, pp.121–2.
2 Friedrich Nietzsche, *On the Genealogy of Morals*, Oxford University Press: Oxford, 1996, I.15.
3 Paul Tillich, *The Protestant Era*, James Nisbet and Co: London, 1955, p.xxxv.ff.

NOTES

4 Roger Scruton, *The Uses of Pessimism*, Oxford University Press: Oxford, 2010, p.17.
5 James Joyce, pp.121–2.

Chapter 13

1 Dylan Thomas, 'Fern Hill', *Dylan Thomas: The Poems*, J.M. Dent and Sons Ltd: London, 1974, p.195.
2 Hal Summers, 'My Old Cat', *The Oxford Book of 20th Century Verse*, Oxford University Press: Oxford, 1973, p.447.
3 Blaise Pascal, *Pensées*, 1670.
4 Philip Larkin, 'Aubade', *Collected Poems*, The Marvell Press and Faber and Faber: London, 2003, p.190.
5 Marguerite Yourcenar, *Hadrian*, Librairie Plon: Paris, 1951.
6 John Donne, 'Holy Sonnets X', *Complete Poetry and Selected Prose*, The Nonesuch Press: London, 1942, p.283.
7 Miguel De Unamuno, *The Tragic Sense of Life*, Dover Publications: New York, 1954, p.263.

Chapter 14

1 T.S. Eliot, 'Little Gidding', *The Complete Poems and Plays*, Harcourt, Brace and Company: New York, 1952, p.139.

Chapter 15

1 Daniel C. Dennett, *Breaking the Spell*, Allen Lane: London, 2006, p.109.
2 Ibid.
3 Howard Jacobson, *Kalooki Nights*, Jonathan Cape: London, 2006.
4 Jospeh Meeker, quoted in Richard Mabey, *Nature Cure*, Pimlico: London, 2006, p.200.
5 Ibid.
6 Alan Hollinghurst, *The Line of Beauty*, Picador: London, 2004, p.500.
7 Paul Celan, 'De Nichts', *Selected Poems*, Penguin Books: London, 1995, p.178.
8 Adam Zagajewski, 'Try to Praise the Mutilated World', *New and Selected Poems*, Farrar, Straus and Giroux: New York, 2002.

Chapter 16
1 J.M. Coetzee, *Diary of a Bad Year*, Text Publishing: Melbourne, 2007, p.3.
2 Thomas Hobbes, *On the Citizen*, Ed. and Trans. Richard Tuck, Cambridge University Press: Cambridge, 1998, Chapter 10, pp.115–6.
3 Coetzee, p.3.
4 Sigmund Freud, *Civilization, Society and Religion*, Penguin Books: London, 1991, p.284.
5 Sigmund Freud, 'The Future of an Illusion', in *Civilization, Society and Religion*, Penguin Books: London, 1991, p.194.
6 Sigmund Freud, *Civilization, Society and Religion*, Penguin Books: London, 1991, p.284.
7 Saint John Chrysostom, Patriarch of Constantinople in the 4th century, quoted in Lawrence Osborne, *The Poisoned Embrace*, Vintage: London, 1994, p.68.
8 Diarmaid MacCulloch, *Silence: A Christian History*, Allan Lane: London, 2013. pp.214–5.
9 Ibid. p.213.
10 Ibid.
11 Coetzee, p.160.

Chapter 17
1 Matthew Tindal, 'Christianity as Old as the Creation', 1773, quoted in Roy Porter, *Enlightenment*, Penguin: London, 2000, p.113.
2 Norman MacCaig, 'A Man I Agreed With', *Collected Poems*, Chatto and Windus: London, 1990, p.363.

Chapter 18
1 'Immaculate Conception of the BVM', *The Oxford Dictionary of the Christian Church*, Oxford University Press: Oxford, 1997, p.821.
2 Ibid. p.117.
3 Ignace Lepp, *Death and Its Mysteries*, Burnes and Oats: London, 1969, p.7.
4 Isaiah Berlin, *The Proper Study of Mankind*, Chatto and Windus, London, 1997, pp 239ff.
5 John Gray, *Berlin*. Fontana Press: London, 1995, p.71.

NOTES

6 Denis Healey.
7 Isaiah Berlin, *Concepts and Categories*, Hogarth Press: London, 1978. p.166.

Chapter 19
1 Hendrik Hertzberg, *Politics: Observations and Arguments*, Penguin Books: New York, 2004, p.xviii.
2 Louis MacNeice, 'Mutations', *Collected Poems*, Faber and Faber: London, 1966, p.195.

Chapter 20
1 Wilfrid Owen, 'Preface', *The Collected Poems*, Chatto and Windus: London, 1963, p.31.
2 Friedrich Nietzsche, *Assorted Opinions and Maxims*, 1879.
3 Wilfrid Owen, 'Strange Meeting', *The Collected Poems*, Chatto and Windus: London, 1963, p.35.

Chapter 21
1 Norman MacCaig, 'July Evening', *Collected Poems*, Chatto and Windus: London, 1990, p.111.

Chapter 22
1 Yehuda Amichai, 'The Place Where We Are Right', *The Selected Poetry*, University of California Press: Oakland, 2018, p.34.

Chapter 23
1 Thomas Hardy, 'The Oxen', *The Oxford Book of Twentieth Century English Verse*, Clarendon Press: Oxford, 1973, p.13.
2 C. Day Lewis, 'Christmas Eve', *The Complete Poems*, Sinclair Stevenson: London, 1992, p.517.
3 John Betjeman, 'Christmas', *Collected Poems*, John Murray: London, 1958, p.188.
4 Edwin Morgan, 'Trio', *Collected Poems*, Carcanet Press: Manchester, 1990, p.172.

PERMISSION CREDITS

'The Place Where We Are Right' by Yehuda Amichai used with permission of the University of California Press, from *The Selected Poetry of Yehuda Amichai* by Yehuda Amichai, edited and translated by Chana Bloch and Stephen Mitchell, copyright © 2013 by Chana Bloch and Stephen Mitchell; permission conveyed through Copyright Clearance Center, Inc.

'Friday's Child' by W.H. Auden from *Collected Poems* (Faber & Faber, 1976) Copyright © 1940 and 1960 by The Estate of W.H. Auden. Reprinted by permission of Curtis Brown, Ltd. All rights reserved.

'Funeral Blues' by W.H. Auden from *Collected Poems* (Faber & Faber, 1976) Copyright © 1940 and 1960 by The Estate of W.H. Auden. Reprinted by permission of Curtis Brown, Ltd. All rights reserved.

'In Memory of Sigmund Freud' by W.H. Auden from *Collected Poems* (Faber & Faber, 1976) Copyright © 1940 and 1960 by The Estate of W.H. Auden. Reprinted by permission of Curtis Brown, Ltd. All rights reserved.

'Christmas' by John Betjeman from *Collected Poems* (John Murray, 1958) copyright © 1955, The Estate of John Betjeman.

'Psalm from the Die Niemandsrose Series' by Paul Celan from *Selected Poems* (Penguin Books, 1995). Translation copyright © Michael Hamburger 1972. Reprinted by permission of The Random House Group Limited.

'Simone Weil at Saint-Marcel d'Ardèche' by James Charlton from *So Much Light* (Pardalote Press, 2007). Reproduced by permission of James Charlton.

'Old Woman' by Iain Crichton Smith from *New Collected Poems* (Carcanet, 2011) reprinted by kind permission of Carcanet Press, Manchester, UK.

'Christmas Eve' by Cecil Day Lewis from *The Complete Poems* (Sinclair-Stevenson, 1992) Copyright © 1992 The Estate of C. Day Lewis. Reprinted by permission of The Random House Group Limited.

'Little Gidding' by T.S. Eliot from *The Complete Poems and Plays*, (Harcourt, Brace and Company, 1952). Reproduced by permission of Faber & Faber Ltd.

'Aubade' by Philip Larkin from *Collected Poems* (The Marvell Press and Faber and Faber Ltd. 2003). Reproduced by permission of Faber & Faber Ltd.

ON REFLECTION

'A Man I Agreed With' by Norman MacCaig from *The Poems of Norman MacCaig* (Polygon (An Imprint of Birlinn Limited), 2009) copyright © the estate of Norman McCaig. Reproduced with permission of Birlinn Ltd through PLSclear.

'July Evening' by Norman MacCaig from *The Poems of Norman MacCaig* (Polygon (An Imprint of Birlinn Limited), 2009) copyright © the estate of Norman McCaig. Reproduced with permission of Birlinn Ltd through PLSclear.

'Mutations' by Louis MacNeice from *Collected Poems* (Faber & Faber Ltd, 2016). Reproduced by permission of Faber & Faber Ltd.

'Trio' by Edwin Morgan from *Centenary Selected Poems* (Carcanet, 2020) reprinted by kind permission of Carcanet Press, Manchester, UK.

'Going Without Saying' by Bernard O'Donoghue reproduced by permission of Bernard O'Donoghue.

'My Old Cat' by Hal Summers. Copyright © The Estate of Hal Summers.

'Try to Praise the Mutilated World' by Adam Zagajewski, translated by Claire Cavanaugh from *Without End: New and Selected Poems*. Copyright © 2002 by Adam Zagajewski. Translation copyright © 2002 by Farrar, Straus and Giroux. Reprinted/used by permission of Farrar, Straus and Giroux, and Faber and Faber, Ltd. All rights reserved.